DOCUMENTING HISTORY

WORLD WAR II
1939–45

CHRISTINE HATT

FRANKLIN WATTS

A Division of Scholastic Inc.

NEW YORK TORONTO LONDON AUCKLAND SYDNEY

MEXICO CITY NEW DELHI HONG KONG

DANBURY, CONNECTICUT

First published by Evans Brothers Limited, 2000
2A Portman Mansions
Chiltern Street
London
W1M ILE

© Evans Brothers Limited 2000

First American edition 2001 by Franklin Watts
A Division of Scholastic Inc.
90 Sherman Turnpike
Danbury, CT 06816

Catalog details are available from the Library of Congress
Cataloging-in-Publication Data

Printed in Spain by GRAFO

Design – Neil Sayer
Editorial – Nicola Barber
Maps – Tim Smith
Consultant – Terry Charman, Historian in the Research and
Information Office, Imperial War Museum, London
Production – Jenny Mulvanny

Title page picture: The Battle of Kursk, 1943
Border: Concentration camp watchtowers and barbed wire

ISBN 0-531-14612-X (Lib. Bdg.)

ACKNOWLEDGMENTS

For permission to reproduce copyright pictorial material, the author and
publishers gratefully acknowledge the following:

cover (top left) the art archive (top right) Topham Picturepoint (bottom left) the
art archive (bottom right) Hulton Getty **page 7** Popperfoto **page 8** e.t. archive
page 9 (left) Topham Picturepoint (right) Mary Evans Picture Library **page 11**
Mary Evans Picture Library **page 12** Popperfoto **page 13** (top left) e.t. archive
(top right) Mary Evans/Explorer Archives (bottom) Popperfoto **page 14** (top)
e.t. archive (bottom) Mary Evans Picture Library **page 15** (top) Mary Evans
Picture Library (bottom) Popperfoto **page 16** Topham Picturepoint **page 17**
(top) Mary Evans Picture Library (bottom) Topham Picturepoint **page 18** (top)
e.t. archive (bottom) Popperfoto **page 19** Mary Evans Picture Library **page 21**
Topham Picturepoint **page 22** (left) Hulton Getty (right) e.t.archive **page 23**
Popperfoto **page 24** (top) Mary Evans Picture Library (bottom) Topham
Picturepoint **page 25** (top) e.t. archive (bottom) Popperfoto **page 26** Hulton
Getty **page 27** Topham Picturepoint **page 28** e.t. archive **page 29** (top) e.t.
archive (bottom) Topham Picturepoint **page 31** (top) Topham Picturepoint
(bottom) Topham Picturepoint **page 32** Mary Evans Picture Library **page 33**
(top) Mary Evans/Alexander Meledin Collection (bottom) Topham Picturepoint
page 35 e.t. archive **page 37** e.t. archive **page 38** Hulton Getty **page 39**
Topham Picturepoint **page 40** (top) Topham Picturepoint (bottom) Popperfoto
page 41 (left) Hulton Getty (right) Topham Picturepoint **page 42** (top)
Topham Picturepoint (bottom) Mary Evans Picture Library **page 43** Hulton
Getty **page 44** Hulton Getty **page 46** Topham Picturepoint **page 47** Topham
Picturepoint **page 48** (top) Topham Picturepoint (bottom) Topham Picturepoint
page 49 Imperial War Museum **page 51** Topham Picturepoint **page 52**
Topham Picturepoint **page 53** Topham Picturepoint **page 54** e.t. archive **page
55** Popperfoto **page 56** e.t. archive **page 57** (top) Topham Picturepoint(bottom) e.t. archive **page 58** (right) Popperfoto (left) Topham Picturepoint **page
59** Topham Picturepoint

For permission to reproduce copyright material for the documents, the author
and publisher gratefully acknowledge the following:

page 6, 11, 35, 59 From *The Major International Treaties 1914-1973* by J.A.S.
Grenville, published in 1974 by Methuen & Co Ltd. Reprinted by permission of
David Higham Associates. **page 7, 17, 43, 55** From *The Past is Myself* by
Christabel Bielenberg, published by Transworld Publishers Ltd, a division of
the Random House Group Ltd. Copyright © Christabel Bielenberg 1984. All
rights reserved. **page 7** (top and bottom right) **33, 47** (bottom) From *The
Second World War in Europe* by S.P. Mackenzie, published in 1999 by
Addison Wesley Longman, a division of Pearson Education Ltd. **page 7**
(bottom left) From *Hiroshima* by John Hershey, published in 1966 by Hamish
Hamilton. Copyright © John Hershey, 1985. Reprinted by permission of
Penguin UK **page 9** From *The Storm of Steel: From the Diary of a German
Storm-Troop Officer on the Western Front* by Ernst Junger, published in 1929
by Chatto & Windus. **page 13** From *The Origins of the Second World War* by
Victor Mallia-Milanes, published in 1987 by Macmillan Education Ltd. **page
15** From *The Weimar Republic Source Book*, edited by Anton Kaes, Martin Jay
and Edward Dimendberg, published in 1994 by University of California Press.
Reprinted by permission of the University of California Press. **page 19**
(bottom), **49** (bottom) From *The Railway Man: A POW's Searing Account of
War, Brutality, and Forgiveness* by Eric Lomax. Copyright © 1995 by Eric
Lomax. Used by permission of W. W. Norton & Company, Inc. Published by
in 1996 by Vintage. **page 21** From *The Memoirs of Field-Marshal the Viscount
Montgomery of Alamein* published in 1958 by Da Capo Press, Inc. **page 23**
From *Women's Letters in Wartime. 1450-1945*, edited by Eva Figes, published
by Pandora, an imprint of Harper Collins Publishers. **page 25** From *Memoirs -
Ten Years and Twenty Days* by Admiral Doenitz, published in 1958 by Bernhard
& Graefe. **page 27** Taken from *War Poems* by Christopher Martin, published in
1991 by Collins Educational, a division of Harper Collins Publishers. **page 29**
From *Jahrbuch des Auslands - Organisation der NSDAP, 1942*. **page 31** From
The Second World War by John Keegan, published in 1997 by Pimlico.
Copyright © 1989 John Keegan. Reproduced by permission of Sheil Land
Associates Ltd. **page 37, 51** From *The Good War: An Oral History of World War
Two* by Studs Terkel, published in 1985 by Hamish Hamilton. Copyright
©1985 by Studs Terkel. Reprinted by permission of Penguin UK. **page 39**
From *Midway: The Battle That Doomed Japan* (Tokyo, 1968) by M Fuchida
and M Okumiya. **page 41, 55** (bottom) From *The Second World War and Its
Aftermath* by Colin C Bayne-Jardine, published in 1987 by Addison Wesley
Longman, a division of Pearson Education Ltd. **page 45** From *Children's
Wartime Diaries* by Laurel Holliday, published by Judy Piatkus (Publishers)
Ltd. © Laurel Holliday, 1995. **page 49** (top) From *The Imperial War Museum
Book of Victory in Europe* by Julian Thompson. Copyright © Julian Thompson
and the Imperial War Museum 1994. **page 53** (top) From *The Imperial War
Museum Book of Victory in Europe* by Julian Thompson. Reprinted by
permission of Derrick Vernon. **page 53** (bottom) *Winter in the Morning: A
Young Girl's Life in the Warsaw Ghetto and Beyond. 1939-1945*, by Janina
Bauman, published by Virago. Reprinted by permission of Virago.

While every effort has been made to secure permission to use copyright
material, Evans Brothers apologize for any errors or omissions in the above
list and would be grateful for notification of any corrections to be included in
subsequent editions.

 Personal diaries kept by soldiers in the battle zones offer shocking glimpses into the grim reality of warfare. One German soldier recorded the slow starvation he and his comrades suffered in the ruins of Stalingrad, Russia (see page 33).

December 26. The horses have already been eaten. I would eat a cat... The soldiers look like corpses or lunatics, looking for something to put in their mouths. They no longer take cover from Russian shells; they haven't the strength to walk, run away and hide. A curse on this war!

Private letters are another important source of information about the war. This extraordinary note (see page 55) was written by a Japanese *kamikaze* pilot just before he set off on a suicide mission against an American ship in the Pacific Ocean.

I leave for the attack with a smile on my face. The moon will be full tonight. As I fly over the open sea off Okinawa I will choose the enemy ship that is to be my target.
I will show you that I know how to die bravely.

A young *kamikaze* pilot in July 1944

Many works of literature were inspired by the terrible events of World War II. The dropping of atomic bombs on Japan in 1945 prompted American writer John Hersey to write his book *Hiroshima* (see page 55).

He was the only person making his way into the city; he met hundreds and hundreds who were fleeing, and every one of them seemed to be hurt in some way. The eyebrows of some were burned off and skin hung from their faces and hands. Others, because of pain, held their arms up as if carrying something in both hands.

Transcripts of the War Crimes Trials (1945-46) reveal the thoughts of many high-ranking Nazis. In this interview, the commandant of a concentration camp explained how he carried out mass murder (see page 47).

...it was possible to exterminate up to 10,000 people in one 24-hour period... The killing itself took the least time... it was the burning that took all the time. The killing was easy; you didn't even need guards to drive them into the chambers; they just went in expecting to take showers and, instead of water, we turned on poison gas....

CHAPTER 1

ORIGINS
WORLD WAR I

The tensions that led to World War I began to develop in 1871, when more than thirty small states united to create the German Empire. The new, strong Germany formed the Triple Alliance with Austria-Hungary and Italy in 1882. Wary of Germany's increasing power, Britain and France came to an agreement to help each other, known as the Entente Cordiale, in 1904.

Austria-Hungary ruled a declining empire. Its people included thousands of Slavs, many of them Serbs, who wanted independence. They were backed by the Slavic states of Serbia and Russia. In 1907, Russia joined Britain and France against the Triple Alliance, forming the Triple Entente.

Then, in 1914, a Serb killed the heir to the Austro-Hungarian throne. Austria-Hungary blamed Serbia for the crime and declared war, as did its ally, Germany. Russia entered the war on Serbia's side and was quickly joined by its Triple Entente partners, Britain and France. World War I had begun.

The Allies (Britain, France, and Russia) and the Central Powers (Germany and Austria-Hungary) both predicted that the fighting would be over within a year. But instead, Germany's invasion of Belgium and France led to a stalemate and years of trench warfare, in which millions of men died as they fought again and again over the same territory. As time passed, more countries entered the war. Among them

were Italy (1915) and the United States (1917), which joined the Allies, as well as Turkey (1914) and Bulgaria (1915), who sided with the Central Powers.

The number of fronts increased, too. Men fought not only on the Western Front in Belgium and France, but also on the Eastern Front in Russia, and in Italy, Greece, Turkey, the Middle East, Africa, and the Pacific. The Eastern Front closed down in 1918, when Russia left the war after its Communist revolution. By late 1918, the Allies were forcing the Germans back along the Western Front. Facing defeat in battle and unrest at home (see box page 9), Germany's ruler, Kaiser Wilhelm II, abdicated his power. The new government (see page 14) then requested an armistice. The war ended when the armistice was signed on November 11, 1918.

The victorious Allies had to work out a peace settlement. A conference to discuss its terms began on January 18, 1919 in Paris. It was signed on June 28, 1919 in the grand setting of the Palace of Versailles, just outside the city.

This painting shows American troops on a ship in the English port of Southampton. They were on their way to mainland Europe, where about two million soldiers from the U.S. fought in World War I.

Ernst Jünger was a German soldier who went to war in 1914, at the young age of just nineteen. He served bravely in many battles on the Western Front and kept a diary of his experiences. In 1929, it was published in English as *The Storm of Steel*. These excerpts highlight Jünger's love of his country and his determination to act both with courage and honor.

Ernst Jünger as an old man

THE STORM OF STEEL

FROM THE DIARY
OF A GERMAN STORM-TROOP OFFICER
ON THE WESTERN FRONT

———

ERNST JÜNGER

LIEUTENANT, 73RD HANOVERIAN FUSILIER
REGIMENT

★

With an introduction by
R. H. Mottram

The Germans had fought and defeated the French in the Franco-Prussian War of 1870-1. In so doing, they had won the provinces of Alsace and Lorraine, which became part of the new German Empire.

A **coolie** is a derogatory word for a poorly paid worker from the Far East.

THE "STAB IN THE BACK"

By 1918, war casualties, severe food shortages, and discontent with the Kaiser's regime had prompted demonstrations and strikes in Germany. Army leader Erich Ludendorff used this situation to his advantage. Once it was clear that the final attack on the Allies had failed, he claimed that the army had been "stabbed in the back" by lack of support from the civilian population. He also assured that the new government, not the army, negotiated the armistice. The "stab in the back" theory was believed by many World War I soldiers, including the young Adolf Hitler.

Adolf Hitler was wounded in the World War I. This 1916 photograph shows him (back row, second from right) during a hospital stay in the German town of Beelitz.

We had left lecture-room, class-room and bench behind us. We had been welded by a few weeks' training into one corporate mass inspired by the enthusiasm of one thought... **to carry forward the German ideals of '70...** The war was our dream of greatness, power, and glory. It was a man's work, a duel on fields whose flowers would be stained with blood.

For four long years, in torn coats and worse fed than a **Chinese coolie**, the German soldier was hurried from one battlefield to the next to show his iron fist yet again to a foe many times his superior in numbers, well equipped and well fed. There could be no surer sign of the might of the idea that drove us on.

THE TREATY OF VERSAILLES

The Paris Peace Conference of 1919 was dominated by three men: the French prime minister Georges Clemenceau, the American president Woodrow Wilson and the British prime minister David Lloyd George.

Clemenceau planned to make the Germans pay for the French lives, land and industry they had destroyed. He also intended to reduce their armed forces so that they could never start another war. Wilson had summarized his idealistic goals in a list known as the "Fourteen Points," drawn up in January 1918. He wanted a fair treaty. The shrewd Lloyd George thought that Germany should be punished, but not so severely that it would then seek revenge.

Over the next six months, the details of the peace treaty were hammered out. The centerpiece was Article 231, the "War Guilt Clause," which stated that Germany was entirely to blame for the war and its results. The following articles declared that it had to pay reparations for war damage, the exact amount to be decided by a Reparation Commission. In 1921, the commission set the figure at 132 billion gold marks. Payment was to be made in the form of ships, livestock, raw materials and other goods, as well as in money.

There was more. The treaty disbanded Germany's air force, cut its army to one hundred thousand men and restricted its navy to ships of a certain size. Submarines were banned. It ordered the total demilitarization of (removal of all military forces from) the Rhineland and made Germany give some areas of land to countries such as France and Poland, others to the League of Nations (see box page 11). Other countries were to hold plebiscites (votes) to decide if

EUROPE AFTER THE TREATY OF VERSAILLES

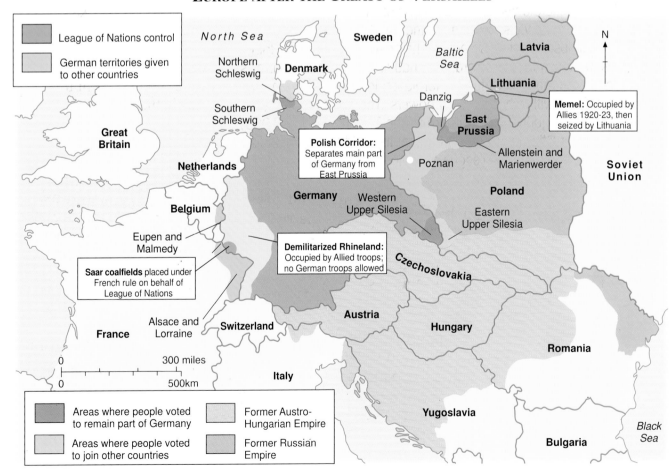

Map legend:
- League of Nations control
- German territories given to other countries
- Areas where people voted to remain part of Germany
- Areas where people voted to join other countries
- Former Austro-Hungarian Empire
- Former Russian Empire

Memel: Occupied by Allies 1920-23, then seized by Lithuania

Polish Corridor: Separates main part of Germany from East Prussia

Demilitarized Rhineland: Occupied by Allied troops; no German troops allowed

Saar coalfields placed under French rule on behalf of League of Nations

Map labels: North Sea, Sweden, Baltic Sea, Latvia, Denmark, Northern Schleswig, Lithuania, Danzig, Southern Schleswig, East Prussia, Great Britain, Allenstein and Marienwerder, Soviet Union, Netherlands, Poznan, Poland, Germany, Western Upper Silesia, Eastern Upper Silesia, Belgium, Eupen and Malmedy, Czechoslovakia, Alsace and Lorraine, Switzerland, Austria, Hungary, France, Italy, Romania, Yugoslavia, Bulgaria, Black Sea

0 — 300 miles
0 — 500km

The main political leaders of the Allies at the Paris Peace Conference in 1919: David Lloyd George (far left), Georges Clemenceau (third from left) and Woodrow Wilson (far right) are joined by Italian prime minister Vittorio Orlando (second from left).

THE LEAGUE OF NATIONS

In the last of the "Fourteen Points," Woodrow Wilson expressed his wish to establish an organization that would promote world peace and cooperation. The first twenty-six Articles of the Versailles Treaty created such a body, called the League of Nations. It first met in 1920, and a year later set up the Court of International Justice to resolve international disputes. But the League was flawed. The U.S. chose not to become a member, while Germany was admitted only in 1926 and the Soviet Union in 1934. Every League decision had to be unanimous, so discussions were often deadlocked. In addition, the League had no troops to enforce its decisions, and members were often reluctant to supply them.

they wanted to remain under German control. Germany also had to give up its colonies in Africa and the Far East. The Treaty of Versailles was signed on June 28, 1919. It was not accepted by the United States, which signed a separate treaty with Germany on August 25, 1921.

Treaties with the newly separated Austria and Hungary, whose empire had collapsed, were also part of the postwar settlement. Both countries were forced to pay reparations, had limits put on their armies and lost land (see map). Austria was forbidden to unite with Germany. More treaties dealt with other defeated powers. The Treaty of Neuilly (1919) reduced Bulgaria's land and army. The Treaty of Sèvres (1920) divided the former Ottoman (Turkish) Empire. Its Middle Eastern lands came under the control of the League of Nations.

These are the two articles of the Treaty of Versailles (1919) that declared Germany's war guilt and demanded reparations.

Belligerency means "being at war."

Article 231. The Allied and Associated Governments affirm and Germany accepts the responsibility of Germany and her allies for causing all the loss and damage to which the Allied and Associated Governments and their nationals have been subjected as a consequence of the war imposed upon them by the aggression of Germany and her allies.

Article 232... The Allied and Associated Governments... require, and Germany undertakes, that she will make compensation for all damage done to the civilian population of the Allied and Associated Powers and to their property during the period of belligerency of each as an Allied or Associated Power against Germany...

THE WORLD BETWEEN THE WARS

People in Britain, France, and the United States hoped that the Treaty of Versailles would create a peaceful world where democracy could flourish. However, in the 1920s and '30s, political instability and economic depression (see pages 16-17) led to the rise of both fascism and communism.

The Fascist movement was founded by Italian Benito Mussolini in 1919. He advocated extreme nationalism — devotion to one's country — and strong government, while criticizing communism and other left-wing movements. Mussolini's strong beliefs appealed to many, and in 1922 he was able to bully the Italian king into making him prime minister (see page 13). A year later, Mussolini's armies invaded the Greek island of Corfu. Far from supporting Greece, the weak League of Nations forced the Greeks to give in to Italian demands. In 1925, Mussolini became dictator of Italy and set about crushing all opposition to his rule.

Fascist ideals also inspired German leader Adolf Hitler (see page 16), as well as other dictators, such as Austrian Engelbert Dollfuss, who came to power during the years between the two world wars. The Spanish Falange Party (see box page 13) shared many Fascist views, especially a belief in nationalism. A strong nationalist movement also emerged in Japan during this era (see page 35), but it did not have one powerful leader.

After its revolution in 1917, Russia, known as the USSR or the Soviet Union after 1922, was ruled according to the principles of communism. The country had only one political party, the Communist Party. Its goal, at least in theory, was to guarantee that power and money were shared among the proletariat (working class), and were not in the hands of just a few land and factory owners. By 1930, Joseph Stalin had become the party's leader. Communists believed that the workers in every country should join together to overthrow capitalism. The spread of communism led to uprisings, including the Spartacist Revolt in Germany (see page 14).

Joseph Stalin (middle row second from right) at a 1930 meeting of the Communist Party in Moscow. He was a ruthless dictator who killed millions in a series of purges.

THE SPANISH CIVIL WAR

In July 1936, Francisco Franco (below right) and several other Spanish generals rebelled against the left-wing Republican government that ruled their country. The Spanish Civil War followed, lasting until March 1939. Franco's right-wing Nationalists were supported by both Hitler and Mussolini. The Republicans received support from Stalin — but not enough to win. After the Nationalist victory, Franco set up a military dictatorship and permitted only one political party, the Falange. The Spanish Civil War provided Germany, Italy, and the Soviet Union with a testing ground for the much larger conflict that was just ahead.

Victorious Nationalists enter Madrid in the spring of 1939 (left).

By 1922, Benito Mussolini's popularity was growing fast in Italy. In October of that year he prepared his supporters (known as Blackshirts because of their uniforms) to march on the Italian capital, Rome. In order to prevent the Fascists from seizing power by force, King Victor Emmanuel III asked Mussolini to form a government. In this excerpt from his autobiography, Mussolini recalls the speech that he made before the march began.

Benito Mussolini (center) and his Blackshirts after the October 1922 March on Rome. The Blackshirts always called Mussolini *Il Duce* (the Leader).

Italy had been on the winning side in World War I, but after the war it suffered serious economic setbacks and political conflict between left- and right-wing groups. By 1922, four governments had been unable to solve the country's problems.

Mussolini was a dictator. However, he did improve transportation and other public services in Italy.

Fascism [marches] against a political class both cowardly and imbecile, which in four long years has not been able to give a Government to the nation. Those who form the productive class must know that Fascism wants to impose nothing more than order and discipline upon the nation and to help raise the strength which will renew progress and prosperity. The people who work in the fields and in the factories, those who work in the railroads or in the offices, have nothing to fear from the Fascist Government. Their just rights will be protected.

POST-WAR GERMANY

After the abdication of Kaiser Wilhelm II on November 9,1918 (see page 8), Germany became a republic, and a provisional coalition government was formed. It was led by Friedrich Ebert, a member of the moderately left-wing Social Democratic Party (SPD).

Extreme left-wing groups in Germany, however, believed that the new government was not revolutionary enough. On January 5, 1919, a communist organization known as the Spartacist League launched a rebellion against the government in Berlin. To prevent unrest from spreading, Ebert ordered groups of ex-servicemen, called *Freikorps,* to suppress the uprising. They did so with cold-blooded efficiency and on January 15 they murdered Spartacist leaders Karl Liebknecht and Rosa Luxemburg.

This poster urged Germans to "Vote Spartacus" — that is for the Spartacist League. By doing so, the picture suggests, they could destroy the provisional government, led by Friedrich Ebert.

On January 19, elections were held to replace the provisional government. The SPD gained the most seats but did not have an overall majority, so it formed another coalition under Ebert. It first met in a town called Weimar because of the unrest in Berlin, so this regime became known as the Weimar Republic. The new government met with as much criticism as the old. It was blamed especially for signing the 1918 armistice and for the hated Treaty of Versailles. In 1920, the *Freikorps* briefly overthrew the government in a coup known as the Kapp *Putsch.*

In 1923, Germany fell behind with the reparation payments demanded by the Versailles Treaty. In response, French and

This illustration appeared on the cover of a French magazine in 1923. It shows French soldiers (on the right) occupying Germany's Ruhr region. Their goal was to force the country to pay its reparations in full.

Belgian troops occupied the Ruhr, Germany's most important industrial region. Germans in the area resisted by refusing to work. As coal mines and iron foundries ground to a halt, the country's already serious economic problems got much worse. The value of Germany's currency (the mark) plunged, while inflation soared.

Germany's government slowly brought the situation under control. In September 1923, the Chancellor, Gustav Stresemann, ordered the people of the Ruhr back to work. In November, financial difficulties eased when the new Rentenmark currency was introduced. (It was soon replaced by the Reichsmark.) In 1924, Stresemann, by then Foreign Minister, signed the Dawes Plan. Under the terms of this plan the United States and other countries lent Germany £40 million, and reparation payments were tremendously reduced.

Further improvements followed. In the 1925 Locarno treaties, Germany accepted its new western borders, abandoning its claim to Alsace, Lorraine and other territories that it had lost. As a result, it was permitted to join the League of Nations in 1926. The Young Plan of 1929 cut reparations still further and the future seemed bright.

THE BEER HALL *PUTSCH*

Amid the chaos of 1923, the German government faced another *putsch* (revolt). It was organized by the National Socialist German Workers' (Nazi) Party, led by Adolf Hitler (see pages 16-17). On November 8, he and six hundred storm troopers from his private army, the *Sturmabteilung* (SA), barged into a meeting at a Munich beer hall. Hitler then tried to persuade local leaders in the hall to back his attempt to seize power. At first, he seemed to win their support, but the next day police suppressed the *putsch*. Hitler was arrested and thrown into prison.

Members of the *Sturmabteilung* during the *putsch* of 1923

Count Harry Kessler witnessed the ceremony on August 21, 1919 in which Friedrich Ebert (right) became the first President of the Weimar Republic. In this excerpt from his diaries, Kessler describes the scene.

They were black, red, and gold.

The **revolution** referred to is the overthrow of the Kaiser and the establishing of the republic.

The stage was festively decorated with the new German colors and plants, gladioli and chrysanthemums...The organ played and everyone in their black jackets crowded between the plants like guests at a better-class wedding... After an organ prelude, Ebert appeared on the stage in a frock-coat, small, broad-shouldered, with gold-rimmed spectacles... Ebert spoke the words of the oath in quite a pleasing voice... the whole occasion had something touching and, above all, tragic about it. This petty drama as conclusion to the tremendous events of the war and the revolution!

THE RISE OF HITLER

In October 1929, Germany's shaky recovery came to an end. The Wall Street Crash in the United Sates (see box page 17) set off a worldwide economic downslide. In Germany, it paved the way for Adolf Hitler's rise to power.

The German economy was hit hard by the Depression. The inflation of the early 1920s returned, making savings and stocks almost worthless. Unemployment numbers rose rapidly, reaching more than eight million by 1932. To make matters worse, the United States could not continue to lend Germany the money due under the Dawes Plan (see page 15).

The coalition government in Weimar could not resolve the economic crisis. So, in 1930, President Paul von Hindenburg took over, using emergency powers granted him by the constitution, and appointed Heinrich Brüning as chancellor. Still the situation did not improve, and in desperation many Germans turned to more extreme politicians. After the elections of September 1930, the number of Nazi Party seats in the *Reichstag* (German parliament) rose from twelve to 107.

During the next three years, a succession of chancellors failed to end Germany's economic chaos. However the popularity of the Nazi Party, led by Hitler after his release from prison, grew steadily. In the elections of July 1932, the Nazi Party became the largest in the *Reichstag*. President von Hindenburg was cautious about Nazi beliefs, but was finally persuaded to appoint Hitler as chancellor in January 1933.

Hitler called an election for March 5, hoping to increase further the number of Nazis in parliament. To guarantee success, he ordered the SA to intimidate communist and other opponents, and banned all press criticism of the Nazi Party. When the *Reichstag* burned down on February 27, the fire was blamed on communists, allowing Hitler to stir up people's fear of a left-wing revolt. But although the Nazis won 288 *Reichstag* seats, they still did not have an overall majority in parliament.

Now Hitler completely took power. On March 23, the Enabling Act was passed, allowing the Nazi leader and his cabinet to make laws without the approval of parliament or the president. The democratic Weimar Republic had ended. All political parties except the Nazi Party were banned.

By 1932, about half of the workforce in Germany was unemployed. People were reduced to searching through garbage dumps to look for wood or other fuel to burn on their fires, and sometimes even for food.

Adolf Hitler greets ecstatic supporters at a rally in the German city of Nuremberg, 1933. While in prison after the Beer Hall *Putsch* (see page 15), Hitler wrote a book called *Mein Kampf* (*My Struggle*) (left). It told the story of his life and outlined his ideas.

THE WALL STREET CRASH

The American economy was booming after World War I. Factories churned out consumer goods for an eager public with lots of money to spend. Stock prices soared and investors on Wall Street in New York grew rich. But by the late 1920s, factories were producing more goods than they could sell, so profits and stock prices slumped. In October 1929, thousands of investors rushed to sell their stocks before their value went down too much. But the frantic trading made prices plummet even faster. The Wall Street Crash continued until November, but the Great Depression that followed lasted for more than a decade.

In 1934, a young Englishwoman named Christabel married a German lawyer and settled in Germany. In her autobiography, *The Past Is Myself* (1968), Christabel Bielenberg explains why she believed Hitler was able to seize power.

What had Hitler provided which seemed to satisfy so many and persuaded them so easily to relinquish their freedom and to turn aside from the still small voice of conscience?... Work for the unemployed, an army for the generals, a phoney religion for the gullible, a loud, insistent and not unheeded voice in international affairs for those who still smarted under the indignity of a lost war: there were also detention camps and carefully broadcast hints of what might be in store for anyone who had **temerity** enough to enquire into his methods too closely...

Temerity means "boldness."

Christabel Bielenberg in 1988

THE ROAD TO WAR

On August 2, 1934, German president Paul von Hindenburg died. Adolf Hitler then added the duties of president to his own as chancellor. To indicate his special role, he gave himself a new title — *Führer* (leader). Now he was completely in charge of his Nazi regime, the Third Reich.

Hitler quickly put his plans for Germany into action. He tackled unemployment at home by launching job-creating plans such as the building of highways. At the same time, he turned his attention to other countries. In *Mein Kampf* (see page 17), Hitler had stated his wish to create a Greater Germany. It was to provide *Lebensraum* (living space) for all the Germans of Europe, including those who had been under foreign rule since the Versailles Treaty.

To achieve his goals, Hitler needed to overturn the Treaty of Versailles. Already in 1933, he had left the League of Nations and had secretly begun to build up Germany's armed forces. He publicly rejected the disarmament clauses of the Versailles Treaty and introduced conscription (compulsory military service) in 1935. Then, in 1936, he sent troops into the demilitarized Rhineland (see map page 10) and established an informal alliance with Italy known as the Rome-Berlin Axis.

Britain and France responded to Hitler's actions

This poster commemorates Germany's annexation of Austria in 1938.

with a policy of appeasement, since neither country wanted to provoke a war. In response, Hitler became even more daring. In March 1938 he occupied Austria, and declared its *Anschluss* (annexation). Next he demanded the return of the Sudetenland, a part of Czechoslovakia where 2.5 million Germans lived. Still anxious to keep the peace, Britain and France persuaded the Czechs to meet Hitler's demands.

After occupying the Sudetenland on October 1, 1938, Hitler insisted that he would claim no more land. But in March 1939, his troops occupied other areas of Czechoslovakia. Britain and France now saw that appeasement was not working. They knew that Poland was another target for Hitler, since he wanted to retake the Polish Corridor lost at Versailles (see page 10). So they promised to guarantee Polish

At a conference held in Munich in 1938, British prime minister Neville Chamberlain informed Hitler that the Czechs had agreed to let Germany take over the Sudetenland. Back at home, Chamberlain proudly announced the Munich Agreement, claiming that it meant "peace in our time."

independence. Hitler, meanwhile, continued to strengthen his position. In May, Germany and Italy signed a military alliance known as the Pact of Steel, in which each country guaranteed to help defend the other in case of attack. In August, Germany and the Soviet Union signed the Nazi-Soviet Pact, agreeing not to fight each other. On September 1, Hitler finally invaded Poland. Britain and France declared war two days later.

Sudetenland Germans welcome Nazi troops in a cover illustration from an Italian magazine, published in 1938.

THE "NIGHT OF THE LONG KNIVES"

Hitler was prepared to do almost anything to gain power in the early 1930s. He realized that he could rule successfully only with the support of the army, whose generals hated the bullying tactics of the SA (see page 15). So he ordered the murder of the SA leader, Ernst Röhm, and of many more SA members. The killings took place on June 30, 1934, which became known as the "Night of the Long Knives."

In Berlin on September 26, 1938, Hitler made a chilling speech about the Sudetenland question. This excerpt is taken from it.

Eduard Benes was the president of Czechoslovakia.

I desire to state before the German people that with regard to the problem of the Sudeten Germans my patience is now at an end! I have made **Mr Benes** an offer... The decision now lies in his hands: Peace or War! He will either accept this offer and now give to the Germans their freedom or we will go and fetch this freedom for ourselves... In this hour the whole German people will unite with me! It will feel my will to be its will...

Chamberlain was the British prime minister.

Eric Lomax joined the Royal Corps of Signals in May 1939. In September 1939, he was based in Edinburgh Castle, Scotland. In this excerpt from his autobiography, *The Railway Man* (1995), he tells what happened when war finally broke out.

In the barracks we had radios on all the time... At 11.00 am on 3rd September, we heard **Arthur Neville Chamberlain** say in his exquisite reedy voice that we were now at war with Germany. Fifteen minutes later, the air raid sirens sounded throughout Edinburgh. From Mills Mount I could look down into the main streets of the city. On Princes Street, the trams came to a standstill; every motor vehicle stopped where it was. Passengers walked with a swift nervous urgency, making for the air raid shelters... It was empty and silent now. Within minutes the streets were deserted except for the immobilized vehicles... A hand had swept over the city, stopping its heart: the war came in this silence.

CHAPTER 2
WAR IN EUROPE 1939-43
THE GERMAN OFFENSIVE

Using *Blitzkrieg* tactics (speed, surprise, and mobility), the Germans quickly occupied most of western Poland. As Hitler and Stalin had agreed in the Nazi-Soviet Pact (see page 19), eastern Poland was invaded and occupied by the Soviet Union. The last Polish soldiers surrendered on October 5.

During the following winter and into the spring of 1940, the Allies were on alert for Germany to make its next move. But although there was open warfare on and under the Atlantic Ocean (see pages 24-25),

nothing happened on land. When no further invasions occurred and no bombs fell, people began to call this era of apparent normalcy "the Phony War."

Finally, in April 1940, Hitler launched his next offensive. He made his main target Norway for two reasons — to establish naval and air bases and to secure the sea route to Sweden, which provided Germany with much-needed iron ore. He planned to occupy Denmark at the same time. German troops overtook both countries on April 9. The Danes

GERMAN CAMPAIGNS 1938-40

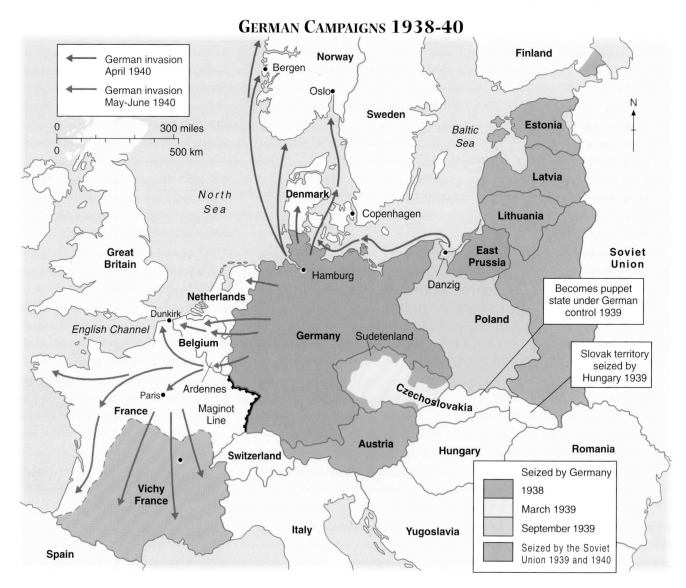

German invasion April 1940

German invasion May-June 1940

0   300 miles
0   500 km

Becomes puppet state under German control 1939

Slovak territory seized by Hungary 1939

Seized by Germany
1938
March 1939
September 1939
Seized by the Soviet Union 1939 and 1940

surrendered almost at once in the face of this unexpected attack. The Norwegians, with British and French support, held out until mid-June.

By this time another German offensive, code named *Fall Gelb* (Case Yellow), had begun. It began on May 10 with the air attack of Belgium and the Netherlands. Paratroopers then landed and ground forces invaded. The Belgians were forced to retreat and the Dutch surrendered on May 14. The French army and the British Expeditionary Force advanced east to meet the enemy.

Next, the Germans began their drive into France. Most of the army invaded through the Ardennes region of Belgium, avoiding the Maginot Line where many French troops were based. The Germans then advanced quickly while the Allies retreated to the Channel coast in England. On May 26, Operation Dynamo, the evacuation of British, French,

Germans seize Kastrup airport in Copenhagen, the capital of Denmark, in April 1940. The country was occupied for the next five years.

and Belgian troops from the beaches of Dunkirk, began. In ten days, hundreds of boats ferried about 340,000 soldiers across the English Channel to safety.

The Battle of France continued as the German army made its way south. Paris fell on June 14

and an armistice was signed eight days later. The Germans occupied northern France and governed it directly. Marshal Philippe Pétain was allowed to set up a separate government in Vichy to rule the south, but only under German control.

By the end of the war, Bernard Montgomery was a field marshal in the British army (see page 57). But at the time of Dunkirk, he was a division commander. In his memoirs, published in 1958, he describes his experiences during the evacuation.

The ships that rescued the Allied soldiers at Dunkirk ranged from navy destroyers to small civilian craft. Many could not come right up to the beaches, so piers were built out into the sea.

A.D.C. is short for "aide-de-camp," a junior officer who works as assistant to a senior officer.

I ordered that any men who could not be embarked from the beaches were to move along the beach to Dunkirk and get on board ships in the harbour. The next night [the] situation on the beaches was not good, for some of the improvised piers we had made began to break up; many had to walk to Dunkirk. While standing on the beach, my A.D.C. was wounded in the head by a splinter of shell. I cursed him soundly for not wearing his steel helmet, quite forgetting that I was not wearing one myself – as he pointed out!...

OPERATION SEA LION

Hitler had seized France fairly easily. Next he began to look farther afield. On July 16, 1940 he issued *Führer* Directive 16, which called for the invasion of Britain. The code name for the plan was *Seelöwe* (Sea Lion).

In this new offensive, Hitler faced a formidable opponent: Winston Churchill. Churchill had become British prime minister in May 1940 after Neville Chamberlain resigned. In the following weeks, with a combination of stirring speeches (see document page 23) and practical preparations, Churchill motivated the British people to fight the expected Nazi attack. On July 10, the *Luftwaffe* began to bomb towns and ships along England's south coast. The Battle of Britain had begun.

The Germans' aim was to seize control of British air space so that their ships could cross the Channel in safety. From August 13, they bombed Royal Air Force bases and radar stations. The *Luftwaffe* made steady progress, but Hitler wanted quick results so that the invasion could begin before winter began. So he ordered the *Luftwaffe* to attack a new target: London.

The steady air raids on London, known as the Blitz, began early in September 1940. The sound of German bombers and the sight of fighter planes — German Messerschmitts, British Spitfires, and Hurricanes — engaged in aerial combat became regular features of life in the city. However the *Luftwaffe* was unable to bring about a decisive victory against the RAF, so *Seelöwe* was called off

LOSING THE BATTLE

In the Battle of Britain, approximately twenty-five hundred *Luftwaffe* aircraft were pitted against just a thousand RAF planes. Many *Luftwaffe* pilots were highly experienced, having fought in the Spanish Civil War (see page 13), while the RAF had a shortage of trained fliers. However, the *Luftwaffe* faced other major problems that led to its failure. Its airplanes could not travel far without returning to base for refueling, and they could not carry many bombs. In addition, their incoming flights were detected by Chain Home (CH), a network of fifty radar stations that had been positioned along the British coast in 1937. As a result, RAF fighter planes knew exactly where to intercept the invaders.

A painting of a Chain Home radar station

The scene after a *Luftwaffe* bombing raid over London. During the Blitz, some forty thousand people were killed and many buildings were destroyed.

British prime minister Winston Churchill visits antiaircraft guns and their operators in London. His distinctive figure, wearing a bow tie and smoking a large cigar, became a symbol of resistance to the Nazi threat.

Winston Churchill knew how to engage the hearts and minds of the British people for the fight against Germany. In this speech, made on June 18, 1940, he rallied people for the crucial task ahead.

on September 17. The Battle of Britain continued into October, when Germany was forced to abandon its plan to destroy British air power.

The *Luftwaffe* remained active in Britain's skies for many more months, however. The Blitz bombing of London was extended to other cities such as Coventry, where the cathedral was almost completely destroyed in an attack on November 14, 1940. Germany's goal now was to undermine morale as well as to wipe out military bases and factories. But the British public was able to keep up its fighting spirit. The Blitz lasted until May 1941. By that time, the *Luftwaffe* had dropped 35,000 tons of bombs on Britain, 19,000 of them on London.

...the Battle of France is over. I expect that the Battle of Britain is about to begin... The whole fury and might of the enemy must very soon be turned on us. Hitler knows that he will have to break us in this island or lose the war. If we can stand up to him, all Europe may be free and the life of the world may move forward into broad, sunlit uplands... Let us therefore brace ourselves to our duties and so bear ourselves that, if the British Empire and its Commonwealth last for a thousand years, men will still say, "This was their finest hour."

The day-to-day experience of the Blitz was extremely difficult, as this letter indicates. It was written by Doll Ratcliff, who worked in London, to her husband Jack, an army captain.

A.R.P. stands for "Air Raid Precautions." A.R.P. wardens had various duties, including enforcing the blackout. This was the covering of windows and doors with heavy curtains at night so that lights inside could not guide enemy aircraft to their targets.

15 Clarges Street
W.1.
Sept. 10th.

My dear Jack,
The last three nights have been absolute hell! We are bombed from about 8.30 p.m. to 5.30 a.m. every night and I have not had more than 2 or 3 hours sleep on either night. I sleep in the afternoon whenever I can but I would just give anything for a quiet night in the country... Everyone is tired out, they say the firemen, A.R.P. and ambulance drivers are beyond praise. The hospitals are packed with casualties and the damage all along the river has been very great...

THE BATTLE OF THE ATLANTIC

As a small island nation, Great Britain was dependent on food, fuel, and raw materials brought by ship from abroad. German warships and U-boats tried to prevent these supplies from reaching British shores as soon as World War II began. The Atlantic Ocean became a battle zone.

From 1939, merchant ships sailed in convoys with navy escorts to minimize the danger from U-boats. Accompanying warships were fitted with Asdic, a submarine-detecting sonar system. Despite these measures, Admiral Karl Dönitz's fleet of fifty-seven U-boats sank 114 Allied ships in the first year of the war.

After the fall of Norway and France (see pages 20-21), the Battle of the Atlantic moved into high gear. Now German shipping could operate from more ports over a wider area. U-boats began to attack in "wolf pack" groups, and to receive support from aircraft, which bombed and spied on enemy ships. By 1941, U-boat numbers were increasing by about twenty per month and Allied shipping losses were growing rapidly.

Britain fought back with more air support and better-equipped escort ships for convoys. Intelligence (see box page 25) helped shipping avoid U-boats altogether. Assistance came from the United States, too. In March 1941 it passed the Lend-Lease

A German U-boat. "U-boat" is a short English form of the German word *Unterseeboot* meaning "undersea boat" (submarine).

Act, which arranged for the loan of money and equipment to the Allies. Many ships were provided as part of the deal. The U.S. Navy also began to escort shipping in the Western Atlantic.

After the United States joined the war in December 1941 (see page 37), many of its warships were sent to the Pacific Ocean. No convoy system operated along the American east coast at first,

though, so merchant ships there were an easy target for U-boats. In the first six months of 1942, the Germans sank 492 vessels in the region.

By 1943 the balance of power at sea had turned against Germany, for many reasons. Improved radar helped vessels to detect and avoid U-boats before they struck. Support groups of escort ships rushed to help

The Royal Navy sank the *Bismarck,* one of Germany's biggest battleships, in the Atlantic in May 1941.

convoys that were under attack. Aircraft carriers accompanied convoys to give on-the-spot air support. American B-24 Liberator bombers were able to strike in sea areas once out of range, and mass-produced American cargo vessels called Liberty ships replaced merchant vessels faster than U-boats could sink them.

By mid-1943, Dönitz realized that U-boats would not be able to win the war by depriving Britain of food and other vital supplies. His submarines continued to harass Allied vessels throughout the war, though, and even in 1945 sank almost 300,000 tons of enemy shipping.

Admiral Dönitz published his memoirs, *Zehn Jahre und Zwanzig Tage (Ten Years and Twenty Days)*, in 1958. In this excerpt, he reproduces a captain's report about a U-boat attack off the Atlantic coast of Africa.

On the beam means "to the side."

Admiral Karl Dönitz is at the center of this photograph, surrounded by some of the naval officers who served under him.

CRACKING THE CODES

While ships and U-boats fought battles at sea, British and German intelligence experts engaged in mental duels. One goal of the British Ultra intelligence unit was to intercept and decode messages containing information about U-boat routes. Its German counterpart, the B-Dienst, tried to discover convoy positions. The Royal Navy code was relatively easy to crack and allowed U-boats to target convoys with some accuracy. The Germans' Enigma code proved more resistant, but progress was made from May 1941 when an encoding machine was found in a sunken U-boat. The German navy code was fully broken in 1942, making it possible to divert Atlantic convoys to safety.

One of the Enigma machines used by the Germans to put secret messages into code

2100 means "9 P.M."

April 30 [1942]. 2100... Found a convoy consisting of some fourteen large, fully-laden ships of between 5,000 and 7,000 tons with an escort of three destroyers and five other escort vessels. Stood off in darkness and a squall of rain... As the escort ahead and on the beam was strong, penetrated into the convoy from astern. Night dark with occasional sheet lightning. Fired six independent torpedoes, depth 15 feet, targets, five freighters and one tanker. All six hit amidships... Dived to 500 feet... Loud noise of sinking ships.

Astern means "from the back."

WAR IN NORTH AFRICA

In spite of its alliance with Germany (see page 19), Italy did not declare war on the Allies until June 10, 1940. The unimpressive efforts of its army contributed nothing to the fall of France. Benito Mussolini (see pages 12-13) then decided that the time had come to make his mark.

Mussolini had long dreamed of creating a twentieth-century Roman Empire. When he came to power in 1922, Italy already had several African colonies, including Libya. In 1935, Mussolini occupied Abyssinia (now Ethiopia). After declaring war on the Allies, he set his sights on British-controlled Egypt and its important shipping link, the Suez Canal.

The Italians invaded Egypt from Libya in September 1940. There were about 250,000 Italian troops, while General Sir Archibald Wavell led only thirty-one thousand British soldiers. However, the Italians were forced to retreat after advancing just 50 miles (80 km). British infantry and tanks stormed after them into Libya.

In February 1941, Hitler sent the Afrika Korps, under the command of Lieutenant General Erwin Rommel, to the aid of the Italians. In March, Rommel began a counterattack, forcing the British back toward Egypt. Although he surrounded the Libyan fortress of Tobruk, he was unable to take it from the defending Australian troops.

In July 1941, Wavell was replaced by General Sir Claude Auchinleck. He launched Operation Crusader, an attempt to end the Tobruk siege and retake eastern Libya, in November. Tobruk was released in December and Rommel was forced west.

The commanding figure standing in the front of this battle-scarred jeep is Lieutenant General, later Field Marshal, Erwin Rommel. His exploits in North Africa earned him the nickname "the Desert Fox."

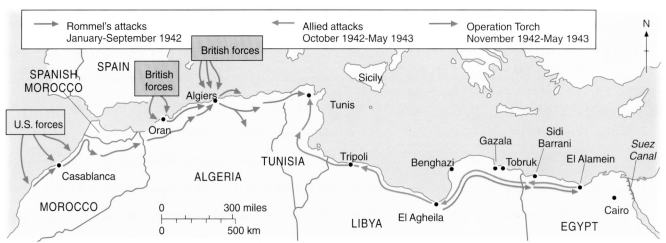

Rommel's attacks
January-September 1942

Allied attacks
October 1942-May 1943

Operation Torch
November 1942-May 1943

N

SPANISH MOROCCO
SPAIN
British forces
British forces
Algiers
Sicily
Tunis
U.S. forces
Oran
Gazala
Sidi Barrani
Suez Canal
Casablanca
TUNISIA
Tripoli
Benghazi
Tobruk
El Alamein
MOROCCO
ALGERIA
Cairo
0   300 miles
0   500 km
LIBYA
El Agheila
EGYPT

NORTH AFRICA 1942-43

British troops at El Alamein in October 1942. The troops' commander, General Bernard Montgomery, predicted that the fighting there would be "one of the decisive battles of history." He was quickly proved correct.

EAST AFRICAN ENCOUNTERS

Britain and Italy also clashed in East Africa. In July 1940, troops based in the Italian colonies of Abyssinia (now Ethiopia), Eritrea and Italian Somaliland briefly crossed the border into the British colonies of Sudan and Kenya. In August, they occupied British Somaliland. The British quickly built up their forces in the region, then struck back. Italian Somaliland fell in February and British Somaliland was recaptured in March. Eritrea and Abyssinia were both taken in April. The Abyssinian emperor, Haile Selassie, returned to power from exile on May 5.

The Germans struck back in January 1942. In June, Tobruk was recaptured and the British fell back to El Alamein in Egypt.

In August 1942, General Sir Harold Alexander replaced Auchinleck, and General Bernard Montgomery took direct charge of the British 8th Army. Montgomery was supplied with more aircraft, tanks and troops, and soon led 230,000 men. On October 23, he attacked at El Alamein. Rommel retreated twelve days later. The Allies had won their first major victory of the war against the Germans and Italians.

On November 8, the Allies began Operation Torch, landing American and British troops under U.S. general Dwight D. Eisenhower in Morocco and Algeria. By early 1943, they were fighting Rommel's retreating troops, as well as German reinforcements, in Tunisia. Meanwhile Montgomery, who had taken Tripoli in January, was attacking from the east. Hitler now realized that North Africa was lost and ordered Rommel home in March. Tunis fell to the Allies on May 7, and on May 13 the Axis Powers in Africa surrendered.

Keith Douglas served as leader of a British tank crew in North Africa and wrote a book and some poetry about his experiences. This excerpt comes from one poem, *Vergissmeinnicht*, in which the writer describes finding a dead German soldier in the desert.

Gunpit spoil means the earth dug up to create a position for a gun.

This is German for "Steffi: do not forget me."

Three weeks gone and the combatants gone
returning over the nightmare ground
we found the place again, and found
the soldier sprawling in the sun.
…
Look. Here in the gunpit spoil
the dishonoured picture of his girl
who has put: Steffi. Vergissmeinnicht
in a copybook gothic script.
…
But she would weep to see today
how on his skin the swart flies move;
the dust upon the paper eye
and the burst stomach like a cave.

WAR IN THE BALKANS

Mussolini also had plans for expansion into the large area of southeastern Europe known as the Balkans. In April 1939, even before the war began, Italian troops had occupied the Balkan state of Albania. As a result, Britain had promised to guarantee the independence of Greece and Romania if they were attacked. But Mussolini was undeterred. On October 28, 1940, he launched a campaign from Albania into Greece.

Italy's armies managed as badly in the mountains of Greece as they had in the deserts of Egypt. By December, the Greeks had forced them far back into

Albania. The Greek ruler, Ioannis Metaxas, rejected Britain's offers of ground troops, both because he felt that they were unnecessary and because he feared that British involvement might tempt the Germans to invade, too. But Metaxas died on January 29, 1941, and by early March, British troops from North Africa were arriving in Greece.

Hitler, meanwhile, was making his own plans for the Balkans. Originally, there were two main reasons for his interest in the region. First, he wanted to secure the area before his invasion of the Soviet Union (see pages 30-31), which stands on

the Balkans' eastern border. Second, he wanted to protect the vast oilfields in Ploesti, Romania, which fueled Germany's war machine. Italy's plight and Britain's arrival in the Balkans made a German invasion seem even more necessary.

While planning his attack on Greece, code named Operation Marita, Hitler won the support of other Balkan states by negotiation. Romania had already joined the Tripartite Pact, whose original members were Germany, Italy, and Japan (see page 36). Bulgaria and Yugoslavia joined the Pact in March 1941. But there was a coup in Yugoslavia on March 27 and its new government rejected the agreement. Hitler decided that Yugoslavia as well as Greece would have to be occupied and brought under direct Nazi rule.

Hitler began his Balkan offensive on April 6. Yugoslavia was soon completely overwhelmed, falling to the Germans on April 17. Greece held out a little longer — Greek troops were forced to surrender on April 23. By April 30 the British forces, under constant attack from the *Luftwaffe*, had completed a sea evacuation to Crete (see box page 29). *Blitzkrieg* tactics had triumphed once more.

Italian soldiers invading Greece in 1940. Much of the fighting took place in mountain areas, where they were no match for the local Greeks.

CRETAN COLLAPSE

Britain occupied Crete in October 1940. After the evacuation from Greece in April 1941, the island's commander, Major General Bernard Freyberg, prepared for a German invasion. The Ultra intelligence unit (see page 25) gave him detailed information about General Kurt Student's plan of attack. So when aerial attack and paratroop landings began on May 20, his forces were ready to fight. Despite staunch defense by New Zealand troops, the airfield at Máleme soon fell. German reinforcements then flew in, and in late May the British had to evacuate again. About twelve thousand men were left behind and taken prisoner.

The remains of an RAF aircraft that crashed during the battle for Crete

German soldiers gaze up at the Nazi flag on the Acropolis. The flag was red with a white circle containing a black swastika in the center.

Athens, the Greek capital, fell to the Germans on April 27, 1941. German archaeologist Walter Wrede was head of the Nazi Party in the city at that time. In this excerpt from the 1942 *Jahrbuch des Auslands-Organisation der NSDAP* (*Yearbook of the Nazi Party's Overseas Organization*), he recalls one of the momentous events of that day.

The **Acropolis** is the high, central area of Athens where the ancient temple of the Parthenon stands.

A **belvedere** is any building from which there is a good view.

A police official comes to the door at 9.30 and tells us that German troops are making their way to the Acropolis. There they will hoist the German flag. I spring to our lookout post on the upper floor. Correct! From the mast of the Belvedere of the city shines the red of the Reich's flag! The cry: 'Swastika over the Acropolis!' rings through the house. In a few minutes we are all gathered together to give thanks to the Führer. The national anthem carries through the now open windows into the streets outside... Flowers and cigarettes are quickly found, and thus prepared we stand at the windows waiting for the first German soldiers.

The **flowers and cigarettes** were to be thrown at the German soldiers as a sign of welcome.

OPERATION BARBAROSSA

In 1939, Hitler and Stalin had signed the Nazi-Soviet Pact (see page 19). For Hitler this was only an alliance of convenience. He hated the communist ideals of the Soviet Union, and thought that its Slavic people were *Untermenschen* — subhumans (see page 46). He also coveted Soviet land, which he wanted as *Lebensraum* for Germans.

The alliance continued into 1940, but tensions between the two partners increased. Hitler believed that the Soviet Union was a threat to Germany's interests in the Balkans and Scandinavia, and he began to make plans for an invasion. In November, when Stalin resisted joining Germany, Italy and Japan in the Tripartite Pact (see page 36), Hitler decided to act. He issued *Führer* Directive 21, code named Operation Barbarossa, in December. By mid-1941, after securing the Balkans, he was ready to invade the Soviet Union.

The Germans launched their offensive on June 22, 1941. It was the largest ground attack ever seen, involving 3.5 million men. German forces were divided into three groups. Army Group North headed for Leningrad, Army Group Center for Moscow, and Army Group South for Kiev. Stalin was taken completely by surprise. His Red Army was unprepared and equipped with outdated tanks and weapons.

The Germans hoped to surround and destroy their enemies quickly. But although the

THE INVASION OF THE USSR

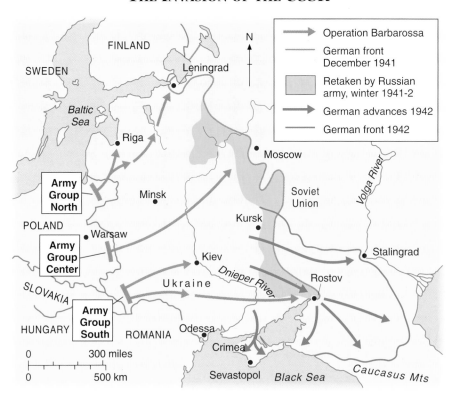

Panzer tank divisions made good progress, the offensive faced major problems. The infantry could not keep up with the tank advance, many tanks broke down and could not be replaced, and summer rains turned the roads into impassable swamps. Red Army resistance remained strong, in spite of severe losses. The army was also able to renew itself by mobilizing more of the Soviet Union's vast population.

By mid-August, Army Group South had captured Kiev. Army Group North reached Leningrad in September and began a bitter siege that lasted until 1944. Army Group Center began to advance on Moscow in October, but its men were exhausted and

supplies were slow to reach them from the far-off border. Soon the brutal Russian winter stopped them in their tracks. Without suitable cold-weather clothing, thousands of men developed frostbite, and the oil froze in their cars and tanks.

The Red Army, however, was used to the icy conditions. On December 6, led by new commander General (later Marshal) Georgi Zhukov, the Soviets were able to launch a Moscow counteroffensive. Hitler ordered his men not to retreat at any cost, but they were forced back. The Soviet capital had been spared, and by spring 1942 there was still everything to fight for.

The German advance into the Soviet Union was swift and without mercy. Soldiers sometimes burned villages before continuing on their way.

In this diary excerpt, a German soldier describes the terrible conditions that he and his comrades endured as they marched towards Moscow in the autumn of 1941.

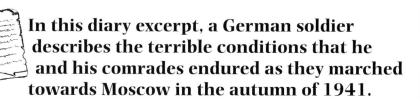

Even in September and before the advent of winter, there was incessant rain and a cold north-east wind, so that every night there was a scramble for shelter, squalid and bug-ridden though it usually was. When this could not be found, the troops plumbed the very depths of wretchedness. The rain, cold and lack of rest increased sickness that, in normal circumstances, would have warranted admission to hospital; but the sick had to march in the column over distances of up to twenty-five miles a day, since there was no transport to carry them and they could not be left behind in the bandit-infested forest. The regulation boots... were falling to pieces. All ranks were filthy and bearded, with dirty, rotting and verminous underclothing; typhus was shortly to follow.

MOVING EAST

Many of the factories that produced tanks, guns, ammunition, and other Soviet war equipment were based in and around Leningrad and Kiev, as well as on the western fringes of Moscow. As the German armies advanced, they seized as many of these vital plants as they could. To save the rest, Soviet engineers dismantled them, then transported them east by rail in a large-scale industrial evacuation. More than fifteen hundred factories were uprooted in this way, and by the autumn of 1941, about 80 percent of the Soviet's military industry was heading east.

While Soviet men fought on the front lines, many Soviet women made weapons and ammunition to help in the struggle against Germany.

STALINGRAD

Once the springtime thaw of 1942 had passed, Hitler and Stalin turned their attention back to winning the struggle for the Soviet Union. The Germans struck first in early May, defeating and occupying much of the Crimea (see map page 30). However, Hitler's main goal now was to capture the industry and oil fields of the Caucasus, which supplied the Red Army.

Hitler launched the main offensive into the Caucasus on June 28. The Germans made quick progress, partly because Stalin had expected an attack on Moscow, so had concentrated his troops there. Then, in mid-July, Hitler divided his forces. Army Group A was ordered to continue south, while Army Group B was sent east toward Stalingrad, an important city on the Volga River. In a separate development, the city of Sevastopol had already fallen to Hitler's forces on July 3, leaving the whole Crimea under German control.

The German attack on Stalingrad began on August 19. During the following weeks, the *Luftwaffe* supported the troops and artillery on the ground with heavy bombing. By September, the German Sixth Army under General Friedrich von Paulus was making its way through the city's burning ruins. It encountered strong resistance from Red Army troops. Each house and factory was defended to the death in hand-to-hand fighting. But by November, when the winter cold was biting deep, much of the city was in the hands of the Germans.

Then came the daring Soviet counterstrike, Operation Uranus, devised by Marshal Zhukov (see page 30) and Marshal Aleksandr Vasilevsky. On November 19, troops attacked not the strong German forces inside Stalingrad, but the weaker Romanians and Italians to the north and south. Tanks smashed through their ranks and within four days the Soviets had encircled the city. A rescue attempt failed, and the *Luftwaffe* could not fly in enough supplies. Soon the three hundred thousand Germans trapped in Stalingrad began to starve.

Much worse was in store for Hitler, as more Soviet gains threatened Army Group A in the

Soldiers fought to the death for almost every building in Stalingrad. The Germans were determined to seize "Stalin's city." The Soviets were equally determined to resist.

Caucasus. The Nazi leader was concerned that the escape route via Rostov would soon be cut off, so he authorized the army's withdrawal in December. He refused, however, to allow the Germans in Stalingrad to abandon the fight. But after suffering more losses in a new Soviet attack, General von Paulus surrendered on January 31, 1943. German dreams of victory in the Soviet Union had received a crushing blow.

Flares light up the night sky above the Kursk battleground, set off by Soviet troops to guide their tanks to German targets.

The following excerpts are taken from the diary of a German Sixth Army soldier. It was found in the ruins of Stalingrad.

Field Marshal Eric von Manstein secured the Crimea for Germany in July 1942 before attempting the relief of Stalingrad.

THE BATTLE OF KURSK

After Stalingrad, the Soviets continued to push west. But Hitler was not yet defeated. In March 1943, his forces staged a successful counterattack in the Ukraine. Next they planned to assault Kursk, where Soviet troops were exposed in a frontline salient (bulge). However, Hitler delayed the offensive until the summer, during which time the Soviets learned of his plan and strengthened their defenses with mines and artillery. When the German tanks moved in on July 5, they met this deadly opposition. Still they persisted until, on July 12, the Soviets counterattacked. The greatest tank battle in history followed, with about seven hundred German vehicles ranged against

about nine hundred from the Soviet army. This brutal armored clash led Hitler to call off his offensive the next day. From then on, the Soviet advance was unstoppable.

November 29. We are encircled. It was announced this morning that the Führer had said: "The army can trust me to do everything necessary to ensure supplies and rapidly break the [Soviet] encirclement."
December 3. We are on hunger rations and waiting for the rescue that the Führer promised...
December 7. Rations have been cut to such an extent that the soldiers are suffering terribly from hunger; they are issuing one loaf of stale bread for five men...
December 18. The officers today told the soldiers to be prepared for action. General Manstein is approaching Stalingrad from the south with strong forces. This brought hope to the soldiers' hearts. God, let it be!...
December 25. The Russian radio has announced the defeat of Manstein. Ahead of us is either death or captivity.
December 26. The horses have already been eaten. I would eat a cat... The soldiers look like corpses or lunatics, looking for something to put in their mouths. They no longer take cover from Russian shells; they haven't the strength to walk, run away and hide. A curse on this war!

CHAPTER 3

WAR IN THE PACIFIC 1941-43
THE RISE OF JAPAN

In the late nineteenth century, Japan began a process of rapid modernization. It did not have enough of its own raw materials, such as iron ore and oil, to use in its new factories. So it started a period of aggressive expansion on the Asian mainland.

Japan built up its empire gradually. In 1904-5, it defeated the Russians, forcing them out of Manchuria in northern China, and stationing troops to guard the South Manchurian Railway. By 1910, it had occupied Korea. During World War I, Japan fought on the side of the Allies and took over more lands in China. After the war, it made plans to increase its territories in China, since civil war had weakened Chinese resistance. But by then the United

States and Britain were on the lookout, aware of the Japanese threat to their own Pacific interests.

The growth of Japan's navy was of particular concern to Western powers. In 1921, the United States hosted the Washington Conference to discuss this and related issues. Three treaties resulted. In the naval armament treaty, all participants agreed to limit their navies. Japan also agreed that its navy would remain smaller than those of the United States and Britain. In the Four-Power Treaty, delegates from four nations agreed not to threaten each other's possessions in the region. In the Nine-Power Treaty, nine nations pledged to continue a policy that gave all countries equal trading rights with China.

JAPANESE AND U.S. TERRITORIES IN THE PACIFIC

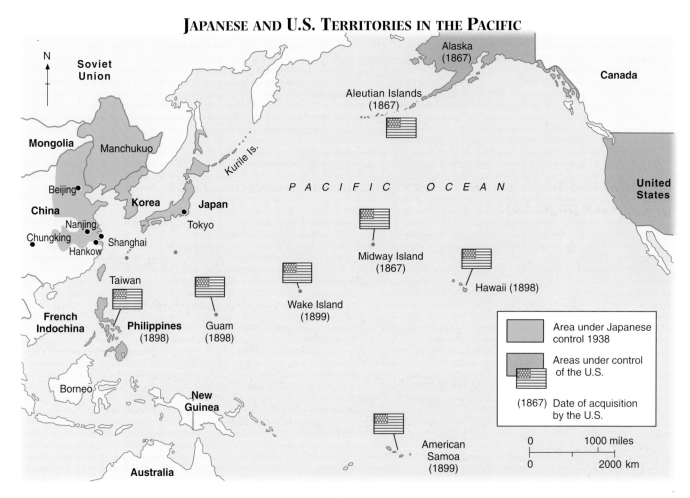

The busy scene at the 1921 Washington Conference

SPREADING SOUTH

Once they had invaded China in 1937, the Japanese advanced quickly. After Beijing had fallen, they moved south to the coastal city of Shanghai. There they clashed with forces led by Chiang Kai-shek, head of China's Nationalist government. Japan took the city in November, after forty thousand of its soldiers and 270,000 Chinese troops had died in the fighting. Nanjing, then China's capital, was occupied in December, so the government fled to Hankow. When the city fell in October 1938, the Nationalists moved to Chungking, which became their wartime capital. By that time, a large piece of land along China's east coast was under Japanese control.

Japan was adversely affected by the Wall Street Crash of 1929 (see page 17). During the Depression that followed, the nation's military leaders became increasingly powerful. They believed that further expansion overseas would ease the country's economic problems and forced the government to act. In 1931, Japanese troops invaded and occupied all of Manchuria, renaming the region Manchukuo. The League of Nations took no real action against the Japanese, but it did publish a report that found them guilty of wrongdoing. As a result, Japan left the League in 1933.

Tension increased as the years passed. In 1935, Japan announced that it no longer accepted the Washington Conference limitations on its navy. In 1936, it signed a cooperation treaty with Germany. Then, in July 1937, it used a clash between Chinese and Japanese troops outside Beijing as an excuse for a full-scale invasion of China. Some historians think that this event, not the Pearl Harbor attack (see page 37), marks the true beginning of World War II in the Pacific.

 The following excerpt is taken from the Four-Power Treaty signed at the Washington Conference on December 13, 1921 (see page 34).

The High Contracting Parties means "the governments who have signed the treaty": the U.S., Britain, France, and Japan.

The treaty was weak because it did not define exactly how it was to be enforced.

Article I. The High Contracting Parties agree as between themselves to respect their rights in relation to their insular possessions and insular dominions in the region of the Pacific Ocean.

If there should develop between any of the High Contracting Parties a controversy arising out of any Pacific question and involving their said rights which is not satisfactorily settled by diplomacy and is likely to affect the harmonious accord now happily subsisting between them, they shall invite the other High Contracting Parties to a joint conference to which the whole subject will be referred for consideration and adjustment.

PEARL HARBOR AND AFTER

THE WAR IN THE PACIFIC

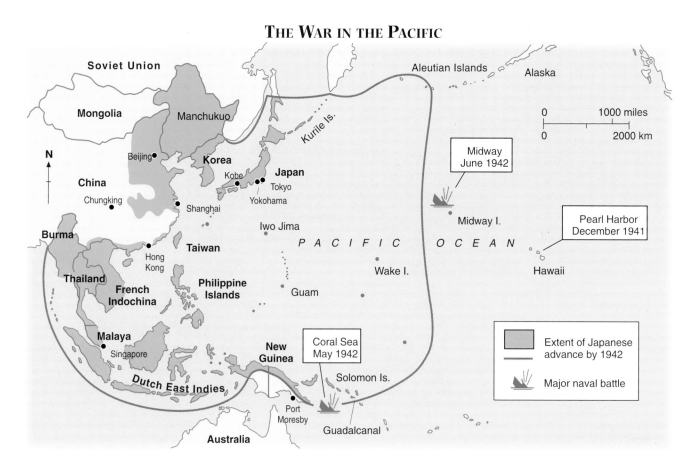

After its success in China, Japan's ambitions grew. In November 1938, it announced its plans for Southeast Asia. Western powers, such as Britain, France, the Netherlands, and the United States, were to be forced out of their colonies in the region. The same lands, with their rich resources of rubber, tin and oil, would become part of a new, Japanese-controlled Greater East Asia Co-Prosperity Sphere.

The situation in Europe soon played into Japan's hands. By 1940, France and the Netherlands were under German control and Britain was busy resisting the Nazi threat. As a result, the Southeast Asian colonies of all three nations were vulnerable to attack. U.S. president Franklin D. Roosevelt realized that new problems were on the horizon so he looked for ways to force a Japanese withdrawal from China, and to protect both American and European territories in the Pacific.

Roosevelt decided to stop Japan's empire-building by imposing economic sanctions. In July 1940, he placed strict limits on the sale of iron and

oil to Japan. This was a serious blow, since Japan was extremely dependent on American imports. But it refused to back down. In September 1940, Japanese forces occupied parts of Indochina, a French colony.

Japan now prepared itself for a possible war in the Pacific. Later in September, it signed the Tripartite Pact with Germany and Italy. Then, in April 1941, it agreed to a neutrality pact with Stalin so that it could concentrate on its plans for Southeast Asia without fear of aggression from the Soviet Union. The United States tried to resolve the situation by extending sanctions and holding talks with the Japanese. Neither measure worked.

In July 1941, tension mounted still further when Japan formally annexed all of Indochina. In response, Roosevelt ended all trade with the Japanese and denied them access to all money and possessions held in the United States. In October, General Hideki Tojo became Japanese prime minister and sent a special ambassador to the United States for discussions. However, American insistence that Japan completely evacuate both China and Indochina was unacceptable. By November there was a stalemate.

The stalemate ended early on December 7, 1941 when Japanese bombers attacked the American fleet at Pearl Harbor in Hawaii. The base was taken completely by surprise — eight battleships were sunk or badly damaged and more than 2,400 sailors killed. On December 8, the United States declared war on Japan. On December 11, Germany and Italy declared war on the United States. World War II had turned into a truly global conflict.

EXTENDING THE EMPIRE

After Pearl Harbor, Japan struck many other Pacific targets. Of the American-controlled territories, Wake Island and Guam fell in December, while the Philippines held out until the spring of 1942, thanks to a strong defense led by General Douglas MacArthur. Britain lost Hong Kong on Christmas Day 1941, retreated from Malaya in January 1942, surrendered Singapore in February and left Burma in May. The Dutch East Indies (now Indonesia) also became part of Japan's empire in 1942.

Smoke and flames engulf American warships in Pearl Harbor after the Japanese attack.

During the 1980s, American writer Studs Terkel traveled across the United States interviewing people about their experiences during World War II. He published their reminiscences in *The Good War* (1985), from which this excerpt is taken. The speaker was John Garcia, from Hawaii.

West Virginia was the name of a U.S. Navy battleship.

I was sixteen years old, employed as a pipe fitter apprentice at Pearl Harbor Navy Yard. On December 7, 1941, oh, around 8:00 A.M., my grandmother woke me. She informed me that the Japanese were bombing Pearl Harbor. I said, "They're just practicing." She said, no, it was real and the announcer is requesting that all Pearl Harbor workers report to work. I went out on the porch and I could see the anti-aircraft fire up in the sky... I was asked by [an] officer to go into the water and get sailors out that had been blown off the ships. Some were unconscious, some were dead. I brought out I don't know how many bodies... The following morning, I went with my tools to the West Virginia. It had turned turtle, totally upside down... We spent about a month cutting the superstructure... tilting it back on its hull. About three hundred men we cut out of there were still alive by the eighteenth day.

THE AMERICAN RECOVERY

Japan's advance into American-controlled Pacific territories had been both swift and shocking. By the middle of 1942, the United States was figuring out how to regain its lost territory. The Japanese were in a dilemma, too. Some military leaders wanted simply to defend their large new empire, while others hoped to increase their territory even more.

Japan finally decided to capture New Guinea, which would give it access to Australia. In May 1942, it prepared to invade Port Moresby, the island's capital. But Magic, the American intelligence operation, had cracked the Japanese naval codes and Admiral Chester Nimitz, now commander in chief of the U.S. Pacific Fleet, knew about the attack in advance. He sent a naval task force, including aircraft carriers USS *Lexington* and USS *Yorktown*, to the region. In the Battle of the Coral Sea on May 7-8, the *Lexington* was lost. But Japan abandoned the New Guinea invasion after one of its carriers was sunk and another damaged.

Admiral Isoroku Yamamoto, commander in chief of the Japanese Combined Fleet, then moved to tackle the United States head-on by attacking the American island of Midway in the Central Pacific. In so doing, he hoped to tempt the remainder of the U.S. Pacific Fleet out of Pearl Harbor and destroy it in mid-ocean. Again, Magic forewarned Admiral Nimitz of the offensive, and again he sent a task force to stop the Japanese in their tracks. By June 1942, Yamamoto had 145 ships in the Midway area, Nimitz a mere fifty. But the U.S. had more aircraft, both on carriers and on Midway itself, and they were eager to win.

The Battle of Midway began on June 4, 1942 when bombers from Yamamoto's four main aircraft carriers raided the island. After Midway-based American bombers struck back, the admiral ordered a second raid. Meanwhile, carrier-based bombers from Nimitz's fleet were headed for the Japanese ships. They arrived as the second wave of

During the Battle of Midway, the Americans lost one aircraft carrier, USS *Yorktown*. It was sunk by a Japanese submarine on June 6, 1942.

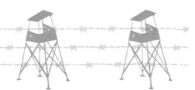

U.S. Marines on Guadalcanal during the rainy season. The Japanese lost about twenty-five thousand men in their failed attempt to hold this island.

THE DOOLITTLE RAID

Many American people wanted to avenge Pearl Harbor quickly. So in April 1942 the government permitted Major General James Doolittle to launch an air attack on Japan itself. The plan was risky. First the aircraft carrier USS *Hornet* moved as close to Japan as it dared. Then long-range B-25 bombers took off from its deck and headed for Tokyo, Yokohama, Kobe, and other cities. Many bombs hit their targets and seventy-one of the eighty airmen involved returned from their mission safely. The Japanese assumed that the Doolittle Raid came from the Midway area. This was one of the reasons they decided to attack the island in 1942.

Yamamoto's bombers, just back from Midway, were refueling and reloading torpedoes on deck. Many American planes were shot down. But enough dive-bombers hit their targets to send three Japanese carriers up in flames. The fourth was hit a few hours later.

The American victory at Midway turned the tide of the Pacific War, allowing the United States to go on the offensive. Its first move was in August 1942 against Japanese troops constructing an airfield on Guadalcanal, one of the Solomon Islands. The Japanese withdrew after six months of intense fighting. The long American recovery had finally begun.

Commander Mitsuo Fuchida led the air attack on Pearl Harbor. During the Battle of Midway, he served on the aircraft carrier *Akagi*. Here he describes the terrifying moment when American dive-bombers began the descent that destroyed the ship. Fuchida was wounded in the raid, but survived to fight again. He became an American citizen in 1966.

Five minutes! Who would have dreamed that the tide of battle would shift completely in that brief interval? Visibility was good. Clouds were gathering at about three thousand meters, however, and though there were occasional breaks, they afforded good concealment for approaching enemy planes. At 10:24 the order to start launching came from the bridge by voice-tube. The air officer flapped a white flag, and the first Zero fighter gathered speed and whizzed off the deck. At that instant a look-out screamed: "Hell-divers!" I looked up to see black enemy planes plummeting toward our ship.

CHAPTER 4

WARTIME LIFE
THE ALLIED HOME FRONTS

Like World War I, the conflict of 1939-45 was fought all-out by armed forces on battlefields, at sea, and in the air. But civilians on the home fronts also felt its effects, and played an essential part in the long struggle for victory.

British civilians quickly adapted to the conflict. During the Phony War (see page 20), about 1.5 million people, most of them children, were evacuated from London and other likely *Luftwaffe* targets. The children were placed with foster parents in the countrysides, but many returned home after no bombs fell. They were sent away again in the late summer of 1940 as the Blitz began. Civilians who stayed in the bombing zones built air-raid shelters at home and some served as ARP wardens (see page 23). A part-time, volunteer defense force was also formed on May 14, 1940, and soon became known as the Home Guard.

Women at work in a steel mill. During the war years, many British women carried out heavy industrial work that previously only men had done.

In January 1940, as U-boats sank food supply ships (see pages 24-25), the British government began the policy of rationing. At first it applied only to butter, sugar, ham, and bacon, but soon other basic items were affected. People supplemented store-bought food by growing their own vegetables. Many also bought supplies illegally on the black market.

Employment also came under government control and thousands of people were sent to work in factories that made weapons and military vehicles. As most British men between the ages of eighteen and forty-one (later fifty-one) were away fighting, much of the burden fell on women. From 1941, single women between the ages of twenty-one and thirty-one had to join the armed forces or sign up for war work at home. Many were employed in industry. Others, known as Land Girls, went to work on farms as members of the Women's Land Army.

People in the United States did not have to go

During air raids, many Londoners sheltered in the stations of the city's subway system. The platforms were crowded and uncomfortable, but they were much safer than the streets and buildings above.

through air raids, but experienced the rationing of items such as gas. American industry, directed by a specially-established War Production Board, contributed greatly to the war effort. Factories built to make military equipment included Ford Motor Company's Willow Run Complex, which mass-produced B-24 bombers. Under the terms of the Lend-Lease Act (see page 24), the United States supplied Britain and the Soviet Union with weapons and vehicles. By 1944, nearly 30 percent of British military equipment came from the United States.

America's wartime industrial growth brought the Depression to an end. However, as the new centers of employment rapidly attracted thousands of people, particularly African-Americans from the South, shortages of homes, schools, and hospitals followed. War industries offered women opportunities for employment in new fields. By 1945, an extra four million had taken jobs.

R-556—Rev. 10-1-42

A

MILEAGE RATION

Americans had to use ration stamps like this to obtain gasoline.

SOVIET INDUSTRY

The people of the Soviet Union endured terrible hardships during World War II. Starvation rations, poor housing and inadequate medical care all combined to make life almost unbearable. But in the midst of the chaos, Soviet industry staged a remarkable recovery after its evacuation to the Ural Mountains and beyond (see page 31). One tank factory was functioning again only ten weeks after its move eastward, and in 1944 the Soviet Union produced nearly twenty-nine thousand armored vehicles.

Nothing was wasted in wartime Russia. Here, Soviet engineers put captured Nazi tanks back together for use by their own armies.

Phyllis Bentley lived through World War II in Britain. In this excerpt from her book *O Dreams, O Destinations* (1962), she describes the many different types of work done by women during those years.

Ernest Bevin was the British Minister of Labor.

...how right Ernest Bevin was when he remarked later that the women tipped the scales of victory. It was not only that 7 million women in the armed forces, civil defence, agriculture and industry, packed the parachutes, typed the forms, drove the tractors and milked the cows, filled the shells, waterproofed the tanks, assembled the radio sets, kept the transport running, put out the incendiary bombs... But it was the ordinary housewife who was in fact decisive. She could have lost the war in any one week. Struggling to feed and clothe her family amid rations and coupons – meat and milk and butter and cheese and margarine and tea and sugar and eggs and soap were rationed, clothes and sweets could only be bought by coupons – if she had once revolted... the whole system would have become unworkable.

THE AXIS HOME FRONTS

The home fronts of the Axis Powers – Germany, Italy and Japan — were transformed just as much as those of the Allies. There, too, civilians suffered food shortages, coped with air raids, and made weapons of war.

Adolf Hitler believed that Germany had lost World War I because its army had been "stabbed in the back" by civilians (see page 9). As a result, he was determined to keep morale high on the home front. In 1936, he began a Four-Year Plan to make the country self-sufficient in producing many foods and preventing the starvation that had killed thousands in 1918. Nevertheless, rationing of meat and other items was introduced in 1939. By 1944, most items were rationed and people had little to eat.

Air raids on German cities began in 1940, and became regular occurrences beginning in 1942 (see page 53). As in Britain, an evacuation program was set up to remove children from the danger zones. It was run by the *Hitlerjugend* (Hitler Youth), a Nazi group that all boys between the ages of ten and eighteen had to join. Many evacuees moved to southern German states such as Bavaria.

Hitler did not fully mobilize the German economy for war in 1939. Many of the available factories were not taken over for military production and the output of weapons rose only slowly. The labor shortage caused by men's departure for the front

Members of the *Hitlerjugend* (Hitler Youth). A special section of this organization was set up for young females between the ages of ten and seventeen, called the *Bund Deutscher Mädel* (Union of German Girls).

was, however, gradually solved by using slave workers from occupied territories.

Change came in 1942, when the Allies threatened German supremacy and Albert Speer became minister for war production. He quickly brought the economy under strict control and output soared. In 1940, German industry produced 2,200 tanks. In 1944, 27,300 rolled off the assembly lines. By then, many women were employed in factories, because they had been ordered to register for war work in 1943. However, the Nazis believed that women's concerns should be mainly "children, church, and kitchen," and there was little pressure to take a job.

Under the rule of Benito Mussolini, wartime Italy

Nazi Minister for War Production Albert Speer tries out a new form of military transport. Speer was also an architect. He designed Germania, the grand capitol that Hitler hoped would be built on the site of Berlin.

grew corrupt, divided, and economically weak. Rationing was introduced to conserve food, but the system was badly run. Italian industry's attempts to contribute to the war effort were also poor. This was mostly due to the government's inability to coordinate production and research, or to keep powerful companies such as Fiat under control. Shortage of raw materials was also a major problem. The production of tanks, aircraft and weapons always remained low, and there was almost no attempt to develop new technology.

JAPAN'S WAR

In 1938, the Japanese government passed the National Mobilization Law, which gave it the power to prepare the country for war. In 1940, a network of local groups was set up to organize a wide range of activities such as civil defense. Two years later, the groups were given responsibility for distributing rations. The Japanese school curriculum was adapted to meet the demands of war beginning in 1941. Children learned about the importance of military activities and about the need to defend the emperor. When heavy bombing of Japanese cities began in 1944, many children were evacuated to the countryside. Japan's war production was small because of its limited amount of raw materials. The country's inability to replace ships and aircraft lost in combat contributed to its defeat.

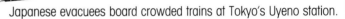

Japanese evacuees board crowded trains at Tokyo's Uyeno station.

Hitler would not tolerate any form of dissent. Special organizations such as the SS (an elite security force) and the Gestapo (secret police) spied on those people suspected of opposing of the Nazi regime. The Bielenbergs (see page 17) opposed Hitler from the beginning, as did many of their friends. In this excerpt from *The Past Is Myself*, Christabel Bielenberg records a discussion with her neighbor, Carl Langbehn, about the SS and its leader, Heinrich Himmler.

For information on the Nazis' racial theories, see pages 46-47.

This means that the SS did not take suspects to court, they just killed (liquidated) them.

Al Capone was an American gangster of the 1920s.

...if it had not been Langbehn speaking, quietly, soberly, without emotion, I would not have been able to believe what he had to say about the SS... and of Himmler who, though he looked like the caricature of any village schoolmaster, was obsessed [with] **fair-haired Nordic types**. Everyone about him, his adjutants, his secretaries, had to be blonde and blue-eyed...The captains of his shining white knights [were cold] clever, utterly ruthless, interested purely in power for the sake of power, they ruled a State within a State, one which had no legal conscience, where the word **"liquidate" had replaced any conception of legality**. It would be useless to appeal to their consciences – they had none. It was as if the **Chicago underworld of Al Capone** and his thugs had been let loose to run the country.

OCCUPATION AND RESISTANCE

Hitler hoped to create a New Order in German-occupied Europe. From France in the west to the Soviet Union in the east, the land was to provide *Lebensraum*, slave laborers, raw materials and food for Germans.

The Nazis governed each nation that was under their control in a different way. Belgium and northern France were occupied and placed under military rule in 1940, while the Vichy regime (see page 21) was set up in southern France. German occupation was extended across France in 1942, but the Vichy government remained. Serbia (originally part of Yugoslavia) and parts of Greece were also ruled by Nazi military administrations.

Other countries were placed under civil (nonmilitary) rule. After their monarchs went into exile, Norway and the Netherlands were ruled by partially independent local governments headed by Nazi officials. In Denmark, King Christian X ruled under strict Nazi supervision. Poland and most occupied areas of the Soviet Union were directly and brutally governed by civil administrations.

The Germans controlled almost every aspect of life in countries under their rule, from education to employment. All

media was censored. Nazi officials supervised industry and agriculture and sent much of their output back to Germany. The economies of the occupied lands were left to collapse and their people to go hungry.

Groups in many occupied areas actively resisted German rule. The French resistance

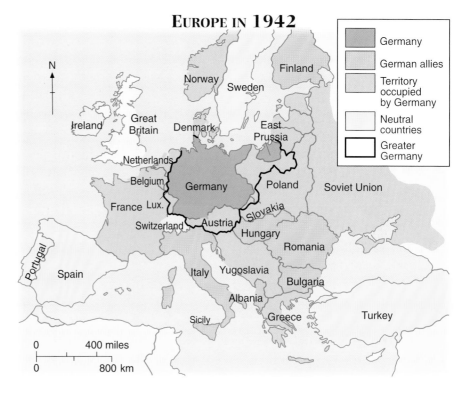

EUROPE IN 1942

■	Germany
■	German allies
■	Territory occupied by Germany
□	Neutral countries
▭	Greater Germany

N

Ireland
Great Britain
Norway
Sweden
Finland
Denmark
East Prussia
Netherlands
Belgium
Germany
Poland
Soviet Union
France
Lux.
Switzerland
Austria
Slovakia
Hungary
Romania
Portugal
Spain
Italy
Yugoslavia
Bulgaria
Albania
Sicily
Greece
Turkey

0 — 400 miles
0 — 800 km

After his country was occupied in 1940, French general Charles de Gaulle escaped to London and set up the Free French Organization. Its members were French soldiers determined to continue the fight against the Nazis. Here de Gaulle inspects a unit of Free French commandos.

movement developed in 1940. It helped Jews and Allied airmen who had crash-landed in France to escape. It also bombed factories, railways and bridges used by the Nazis, and intercepted their radio communications. Resistance was also strong in Denmark, and in 1943 a Freedom Council was set up to organize strikes and acts of sabotage. In Yugoslavia, the anti-Nazi guerrilla warfare led by Marshal Tito was particularly effective. In 1940, the British set up the Special Operations Executive (SOE), which sent agents to support resistance movements abroad. The American equivalent, the Office of Strategic Services (OSS), was created in 1942.

The Nazi stranglehold on Europe was enforced by SS brutality. As a result, most people in occupied countries had to cooperate with some aspects of German rule that they found offensive. There were also a few willing collaborators, who actively supported the Nazis. They included Vidkun Quisling, leader of the Norwegian Fascist Party.

JAPANESE OCCUPATION

The Japanese brutally exploited the inhabitants of China's occupied areas beginning in 1931. But people who lived in the lands that Japan captured after Pearl Harbor hoped for better. The Greater East Asia Co-Prosperity Sphere (see pages 36-37) was supposed to bring an end to Western colonial rule, as well as economic success. Instead it brought domination by the Tokyo government and the diversion of precious raw materials to Japan. Thousands of Burmese and Thai civilians were forced to work under terrible conditions to build the infamous Burma Railway, an important communications link. Europeans were locked up in filthy camps. Any resistance was brutally crushed by the *Kempeitai*, the Japanese secret police.

Many resistance workers paid for their courage with their lives. Among them was a young Dane named Kim Malthe-Bruun. In 1941, he had become a merchant seaman, and on his travels had witnessed the Nazis terrible treatment of the Jews. He joined the Danish resistance in 1944, but was captured the next year. These excerpts come from his prison diary. They take the form of letters to his girlfriend, Hanne.

21 March, 1945

...

The cell I had when I sat in Detention was on the small side – 6 feet, 3 inches by 4 feet – with a small bench and a table. I walked up and down – one and a half paces in each direction; twenty-four hours and all alike, only broken by the opening of the door when two slices of rye bread were handed to me... In the toilet they allowed me to wash, and it was wonderful. Then I paced up and down again, very much surprised that I didn't suffer. I thought of the days spent in solitary confinement and how rewarding they had been. I had the sun, the blue sky... I could smell the earth and feel the coming of spring. It made me choke up inside and I felt very happy... I'm kept going by one thought: that nothing is impossible no matter how black things look at the moment.

4 April 1945

...

Today I was taken before the military tribunal and condemned to death.

Kim Malthe-Bruun, at eighteen

THE HOLOCAUST

Anti-Semitism (hatred and persecution of Jews) existed in Europe long before Hitler came to power. However, the Nazis wanted to achieve something never before contemplated — the extermination of the entire Jewish people. They failed, but not before approximately six million Jews had been murdered in the tragedy of the Holocaust.

In Hitler's mind, Jews were worthy of hatred for many reasons, but he blamed them in particular for Germany's World War I defeat. He also thought that they were racially inferior *Untermenschen* (subhumans), like Slavs. By contrast, he believed in the existence of a superior Aryan race. Its supposed members were all white, often with blond hair and blue eyes.

As soon as the Nazis came to power, the persecution of Jews began. In 1933, laws were passed banning them from many types of employment, including the professions and military service. The 1935 Nuremberg Laws denied Jews the right to be German citizens and to vote. They also made it illegal for Jews to marry Germans. Then, on November 9-10, 1938, *Kristallnacht* (the Night of Broken Glass) took place. Thousands of houses and stores owned by Jews were destroyed, and hundreds of synagogues set on fire. Many Jews were arrested and sent to concentration camps.

By the time the war began, thousands of German Jews had left the country. For those who remained, the persecution intensified. Meanwhile, more serious events were taking place in the newly occupied territories. In Poland, many Jews were killed outright and the rest were forced to live together in special areas, known as ghettos. After the German invasion of the Soviet Union in 1941, SS *Einsatzgruppen* (Special Action Units) went in after the armies to kill Jews, as well as communist leaders. Thousands of people were shot, or poisoned with carbon monoxide in gas vans. But still much worse was to come.

In July 1941, Nazi leader Hermann Goering issued a directive in which he ordered SS officer Reinhard Heydrich to submit a plan for the "Final Solution" of the Jewish question. In January 1942, Heydrich and Adolf Eichmann, another SS officer, agreed to plans for the annihilation of eleven million Jews. Existing concentration camps such as Auschwitz were to be equipped with gas chambers, and new death camps were to be built in places such as Treblinka. The mass killings began soon after. The fit were worked to death. All others were gassed with Zyklon B, and other types of gas.

Since the war, historians have argued about who was responsible for the Holocaust. Hitler and other high-ranking Nazis were certainly aware of what was happening. So, too, was camp staff. But how much the general German public and the wider world knew of the Jews' suffering remains the subject of debate.

After *Kristallnacht* in November 1938, some Germans pause to examine the damage caused to Jewish-owned property. Others simply look away.

Nazi soldiers force Jews out of the ghetto in Warsaw, the capital of Poland, in 1943. The boy with his hands up is believed to have died in the concentration camp at Auschwitz.

FELLOW SUFFERERS

Hitler and his Nazi followers did not persecute only Jews. Thousands of gypsies, homosexuals, and political prisoners died in concentration camps. In addition, about seventy thousand people with hereditary illnesses, children as well as adults, were killed at special euthanasia centers. These were set up after a Euthanasia Order was passed in October 1939.

Eva Heyman was a thirteen-year-old Jewish girl who lived in Budapest, the capital of Hungary. In these excerpts from her diary, she tells how the city's Jews were first herded into a ghetto, then deported. In October 1944, Eva and her grandparents were killed in Auschwitz.

This order was introduced elsewhere as early as 1939.

March 31, 1944

Today an order was issued that from now on Jews have to wear a yellow star-shaped patch. The order tells exactly how big the star patch must be, and that it must be sewn on every outer garment...

May 5, 1944

Dear diary, now you aren't... at home... but in the Ghetto. Three days we waited for them to come and get us... The city was divided into sections, and a German truck would wait in front of the houses and two policemen would go into the apartments and bring the people out...

May 29, 1944

And so, dear diary, now the end of everything has really come. The Ghetto has been divided up into blocks and we're all going to be taken away from here.

After the war, many Nazis were brought to justice at the Nuremberg War Crimes Trials, which were held from November 1945 to September 1946.

The following excerpt comes from an interview given to the official American psychologist at the trials by Auschwitz commandant SS Colonel Rudolf Hess.

The bodies of the dead were burned in huge ovens, called crematoriums.

I asked Hess how it was technically possible to exterminate 2½ million people. "Technically?" he asked. "That wasn't so hard...it was possible to exterminate up to 10,000 people in one 24-hour period... The killing itself took the least time... it was the burning that took all the time. The killing was easy; you didn't even need guards to drive them into the chambers; they just went in expecting to take showers and, instead of water, we turned on poison gas. The whole thing went very quickly." He related all this in a quiet, apathetic, matter-of-fact tone of voice.

PRISONERS OF WAR

Records do not show exactly how many members of the Allied and Axis armed forces were captured during World War II, but it may have been as many as fifteen million. Some fell into enemy hands alone; others surrendered in the thousands. All faced uncertain futures as prisoners of war (POWs).

The treatment of prisoners of war was regulated by several international agreements. One was the Geneva Convention of 1929, which gave prisoners the right to receive food, drink, and medical care, to withhold all information except name, rank and serial number, and to receive letters and packages.

The British and Americans took more than one million prisoners of war, more than half of them German. Some were shipped to the United States and Canada. Many North American camps were specially built in agricultural areas so that prisoners could be employed as farm laborers. After D-Day (see

The ominous-looking Colditz Castle, a POW camp that stood near the German city of Leipzig. Some POWs did manage to escape from its high-security facilities.

pages 50-51), many were also sent to the eighty-six camps scattered all over the United Kingdom. In general, men held in these countries were treated well.

The Soviet Union was far less scrupulous about its conduct toward prisoners of war. Information is scarce, but experts believe it ran about three thousand prison camps. There, millions of Germans and others were ill-fed and treated with the utmost cruelty. Some prisoners never reached the camps. In one terrible

incident that took place in 1940 in the Katyn Forest, near Smolensk, Russia, about four thousand Polish soldiers were massacred by the Soviet security police.

The Germans acted differently toward different groups of prisoners. Their five million Soviet captives were regarded as Slavic "subhumans" and treated accordingly. Many were shot and others were worked to death. Only about 1.5 million survived the war. British, American, and other prisoners were usually sent to camps. There were about ninety camps in Germany, and more in occupied areas such as Poland.

The Japanese took about 145,000 prisoners of war and distributed them in some seven hundred camps throughout their empire. All were treated with barbarity and neglect (see document page 49). Men were fed starvation rations, yet expected to carry out backbreaking physical labor. Medical care was basic or nonexistent. Thousands of prisoners died.

These lines of dejected Soviet POWs stretch as far as the eye can see. The soldiers faced extreme cruelty at the hands of their Nazi captors.

Bohdan Arct was one of many Polish Air Force officers who escaped after the fall of Poland in 1939, then served with the Allies. In 1944, Arct was captured and sent to a prison camp in Germany. While in captivity, Arct compiled a logbook. The two pages (right) and the excerpt (below) are taken from it.

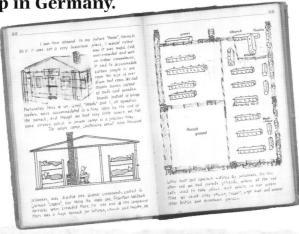

I was then showed to my future "home," Barracks No 11... Cold, overcrowded and with no indoor conveniences, it had to accommodate sixteen people in one room the size of [a] medium bedroom. We had double bunks instead of beds and wooden boards instead of springs... The whole camp... was divided into several compounds... On one end of the compound there was a huge barrack for kitchen, church and theatre... On the other end we had parade grounds...

ENEMY ALIENS

Not all wartime prisoners were members of the armed forces. Many were civilians who, after war began, found themselves living in countries that classified them as enemies. Many thousands of Germans and other "enemy aliens" were sent to internment camps in Britain, but by the summer of 1942 only about five thousand remained under guard. In the United States there were about 110,000 Japanese-Americans living on the Pacific coast. In 1942, all were imprisoned in detention centers, although many were released before the end of the war. Some joined the U.S. armed forces and went on to become highly respected and greatly decorated.

After the fall of Singapore (see page 37), Eric Lomax was imprisoned by the Japanese. At first he was placed in a good camp, but after he was found to have a radio and a railway map, he was brutally beaten and moved into a prison hutch. These extracts from *The Railway Man* (see page 19) describe both experiences.

Our single long hut could hold about a hundred men and was little more than ingenious tents made from local vegetation... The floor was trodden earth... but under each bed-space was still raw clay, which sprouted even in the dark... The cool dark spaces also sheltered wriggling and crawling life, of which the most terrifying were scorpions and snakes...

The left-hand side of the yard was bounded by a wall; and along part of its length were blocks of little hutch-like cells or cages. They resembled drawers in a filing cabinet. We were each ushered into one of these cells through a small, low door about two feet square... I lay down on the floor, diagonally... I had to lie cramped, my arms held up to prevent my own weight crushing the **unset bones**...

A beating had left Lomax with broken forearms.

CHAPTER 5

THE ROAD TO VICTORY
OPERATION OVERLORD

By 1943, Allied victories in North Africa (see pages 26-27) and Stalingrad (see pages 32-33) had overshadowed the Germans' early *Blitzkrieg* triumphs. Next, Britain and the United States planned to bring the war back to Western Europe, and to deal Hitler a final crushing blow.

The Americans had for a while wanted to open a Second Front in France. However, British prime minister Winston Churchill, fearful of another Dunkirk (see page 21), did not want to go on until he was sure of success. In January 1943, Churchill met President Roosevelt at a conference in Casablanca. There he persuaded the Americans to invade the Italian island of Sicily (see box). But the Soviets, who had also been calling for a new Western Front to ease the pressure on the Eastern Front, joined the United States in pushing for action. Finally, Churchill agreed to try for an invasion of France, which

became known as Operation Overlord, in May 1944.

During the following months, every detail of the invasion was planned. American general Dwight D. Eisenhower, the Supreme Allied Commander in charge of the entire operation, worked closely with British general Bernard Montgomery (see page 21), who was to lead the forces on the ground. By early 1944, the basic outline of Overlord was in place. British, American, and Canadian troops were to land on five beaches in Normandy, northwest France (see map), from the sea, and from the air. The invasion was to begin on June 5: D-Day.

When the time came, bad weather caused a delay and the D-Day landings actually began on June 6. About twenty-three thousand paratroopers went in first, followed by 130,000 men in five divisions on the ground. The American forces at Omaha Beach faced strong resistance, but finally got ashore like everyone

OPERATION OVERLORD

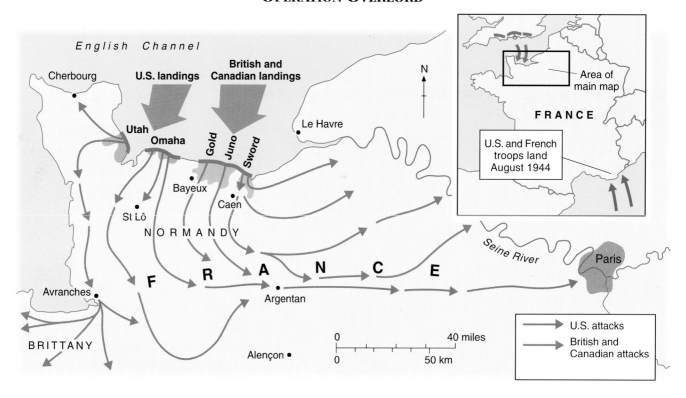

American soldiers make their way through the water to the Normandy coast. The invasion fleet ships (in the background) were too large to come up to the beach.

THE ITALIAN CAMPAIGN

The Allied invasion of Sicily was launched from North Africa in July 1943. Over the next month, the Italians and Germans were forced to retreat, but many escaped to mainland Italy. Meanwhile, Italian king Victor Emmanuel III had forced Mussolini to resign. On September 3, the Italian government signed an armistice with the Allies, but Mussolini set up a separate German-backed government in the north. The Allies invaded Italy from the southern port of Salerno on September 9. They made slow progress and more landings at Anzio in January 1944 did little to help. In May, Allied troops finally took the long-contested hilltop site of Monte Cassino. Rome fell on June 4 and the Germans retreated north, but the Allies did not achieve complete victory until May 1945. By then Mussolini was dead. He had been shot by Italians in April while fleeing to Switzerland.

else. Careful planning, courageous fighting and a false information campaign that led the Germans to believe that the invasion was planned to land near Calais, not in Normandy, made Operation Overlord a success.

Thousands more Allied troops crossed the English Channel during the weeks that followed. Meanwhile, armies led by Montgomery and American generals Omar Bradley and George Patton set out to break the German defenses in Normandy. This took longer than expected, but, on August 16, Hitler ordered his troops to retreat and the Allies moved across northern France. Paris was liberated by a Franco-American force on August 25. In a separate development on August 15, American and French troops had landed on France's south coast and made their way north. Victory was in sight, but it would not be sealed for some time to come.

Elliott Johnson served with the American Fourth Infantry Division. On June 6, 1944 he arrived in Normandy by sea, as he recalls in this account taken from Studs Terkel's *The Good War* (see page 37).

I was on an LST, a landing ship tank. It was three hundred feet long. It had a great mouth in front of which was the ramp that let down the smaller craft. I remember going up to the highest part of that ship and watching the panorama around me unfold. In my mind's eye, I see one of our ships take a direct hit and go up in a huge ball of flames. There were big geysers coming up where the shells were landing and there were bodies floating, face down, face up. The LST, as we vacated it, was to become a hospital ship. The boys who had gone first and been wounded were now being brought out...

VICTORY IN EUROPE

While British and American troops were threatening Germany from the west, the Red Army was keeping up the relentless pressure from the east. By the winter of 1944, Hitler's forces were dangerously trapped in the ever-narrowing gap between them.

Soviet troops continued to move west since their success at the Battle of Kursk in July 1943 (see page 33). During the first half of 1944 they ended the relentless attack of Leningrad (see page 30) and recaptured the Ukraine and the Crimea. On June 22, they launched a new offensive, Operation Bagration, that pushed the Germans into Poland. Then, in August, the Red Army began a campaign in the Balkans that temporarily halted the Soviet drive westward.

In the west, the British and Americans were still making progress, but it was slow going. In September 1944, a plan to invade Germany from the Netherlands failed. Then, on December 16, the Germans launched a surprise counteroffensive through the Ardennes region of Belgium and Luxembourg. At first the Germans were able to push forward, creating a bulge in their front line. But the Allied recovery was swift, and in the Battle of the Bulge, the German salient was eliminated.

By the end of January 1945, the Allies were forging eastward once more.

In February, General Eisenhower (see page 50) launched the Rhineland Campaign. His armies were to cross the Rhine River, then defeat Hitler's forces in the Ruhr region of Germany. American troops led by General Patton made the crossing on March 22, with British troops under Montgomery following the next day. The Germans were surrounded and on April 18, 400,000 surrendered. Eisenhower then sent troops to wipe out remaining German resistance.

The Red Army launched a new attack against the Nazis on January 12, 1945. First it pushed into Poland, taking Warsaw five days into the offensive. Then it continued west, reaching the Oder River, just 30 miles (60 km) from Berlin, by the end of February. Troops showed no mercy to civilians, killing and raping as they advanced. The buildup of Soviet forces continued until April 16, when Marshal Zhukov (see page 30) began his attack on the German capital. Fighting was fierce, but by April 25 the city was surrounded. Hitler committed suicide on April 30 and Berlin surrendered two days later. The Germans signed a full unconditional surrender on May 7. The war in Europe was over.

In this dramatic scene, a Soviet soldier hoists the Red Flag of the Soviet Union above the captured city of Berlin. The devastation caused by the last-ditch struggle for the German capital can be seen below.

This bridge across the Rhine was built by engineers of the American Third Army.

WINNING THE AIR WAR

Throughout the war, the Royal Air Force (RAF) and the United States Army Air Forces (USAAF) used tactical bombing to support troops in action on the ground and at sea. But from 1942, another type of air attack became increasingly widespread: strategic bombing. This type of bombing used air power alone to destroy enemy transport links, factories and cities such as Berlin. Strategic bombing missions, the RAF flying at night and the USAAF during the day, continued until the end of the war. Between October 1944 and May 1945, 344,000 tons of bombs were dropped on Germany. About one million German civilians lost their lives in the wartime raids. Experts continue to debate whether such attacks on defenseless civilians were justified.

Many Allied troops made the Rhine crossing by raft. Here British lieutenant Derrick Vernon of the Royal Engineers describes the scene.

Good watermanship was required to drive the raft across the wide fast-flowing river. Each platoon operated for sixteen hours non-stop. Two rafts were maintained constantly in service, signal lamps were placed for continued operation throughout the night... When ordered to cease operations we were very tired. In three days, the company had made about seven hundred round trips across a very dangerous river in flimsy craft. We suffered nine men killed in action, and twenty wounded.

Janina Bauman was a young Jewish woman who managed to survive in Poland until the war's end. In this excerpt from her book, *Winter In The Morning* (1986), she describes the arrival of Soviet troops in her village on their way to Berlin.

Kracow, a Polish city.

The Red Army was now heading westwards with unbelievable speed. On the day that the long-awaited battle of Warsaw finally began, we also heard the first sounds of the Eastern Front approaching Cracow... For us the war came to an abrupt end at 8 a.m. on Friday, January 19, 1945. After a sleepless night echoing with cannon-fire, heavy with great expectations, we saw in the faint light of the wintry dawn the weird, grey hunched outlines of the first Russian soldiers.

Janina Bauman, at eleven years old

VICTORY IN THE PACIFIC

By mid-1943, after defeats at the Battle of Midway and Guadalcanal (see pages 38-39), the Japanese were on the defensive in the Pacific. Their strong fierce resistance to the American advance on Japan itself led to the employment of a new and horrifying weapon of war.

The Americans launched a two-pronged offensive against the Japanese. General Douglas MacArthur was to take New Guinea and the Philippines. Admiral Chester Nimitz was to drive the enemy from the small island groups in the Central Pacific. The assault on New Guinea began in September and by early 1944, the Americans were in control of the island. Nimitz began his attacks in November 1943 and by mid-1944, the Gilbert, Marshall, Caroline and Mariana islands were also in American hands. American forces secured a victory in Saipan, one of the Mariana Islands, by winning the Battle of the Philippine Sea in June.

THE WAR IN THE PACIFIC 1944-45

Key:
→ Allied attacks
● Nuclear explosion
Major naval battles
1 Philippine Sea, June 1944
2 Leyte Gulf, October 1944

In July 1944, President Roosevelt, MacArthur and Nimitz met to decide the American forces' next move. Roosevelt ordered Nimitz to work with MacArthur for the reconquest of the Philippines. Air strikes on the islands began shortly afterwards. Then, on October 20, American troops landed on Leyte (see map). The Japanese navy responded by attacking the American fleet. The Battle of Leyte Gulf, which lasted from October 23-26, ended with the withdrawal of the Japanese and the collapse of their naval threat to the United States. Combat on the islands was also intense. Manila, the Philippine capital, did not fall until March 1945.

By early 1945, the Americans were hoping to force a Japanese surrender. The nearby islands of Iwo Jima and Okinawa were

The devastated landscape of Hiroshima after the atomic bomb fell

taken in the spring. At the same time, air raids on Tokyo by B-29 bombers were intensified. However, it became obvious that Japan was not going to surrender, and might have to be invaded. Allied leaders knew that Japanese soldiers would fight to the death to fight off invasion. The casualty figures would reach the hundreds of thousands.

There was another option. Scientists working on the secret Manhattan Project in the United States had developed an atomic bomb. It was believed to be so powerful a weapon it could force a surrender. Roosevelt had died in April, so the new president, Harry S. Truman, had to decide whether to use this weapon. He gave his approval and a message was sent to Japan on July 27 demanding surrender or threatening to use the bomb. The message was ignored. On August 6, a bomb was dropped on the city of Hiroshima. About eighty thousand people were killed, but Japan's government did not give up. On August 9 another bomb was dropped on Nagasaki. Five days later, Emperor Hirohito announced Japan's surrender.

BACK TO BURMA

The British also fought to regain territories that they had lost to Japan. Among them was Burma. Lieutenant General Sir William Slim launched his offensive from the north in December 1944. As his troops moved south they met strong resistance, but by May 1945 had taken the country's capital, Rangoon.

 During the Battle of Leyte Gulf and on many other occasions, Japanese *kamikaze* pilots flew their airplanes into enemy ships. They chose their deaths for the honor of Japan. This excerpt comes from a letter written by *kamikaze* pilot Akio Otsuka.

11:30 a.m. – the last morning. I shall now have breakfast and then go to the aerodrome. I am busy with my final briefing and have no time to write any more. So I bid you farewell...

Keep in good health.

I believe in the victory of Greater Asia.

I pray for the happiness of you all, and I beg your forgiveness for my lack of piety.

I leave for the attack with a smile on my face. The moon will be full to-night. As I fly over the open sea off Okinawa I will choose the enemy ship that is to be my target.

I will show you that I know how to die bravely.

A young *kamikaze* pilot in July 1944

 American writer John Hersey wrote *Hiroshima* in 1946, a year after the atomic bomb fell on that city. His book contains the stories of six men and women who survived the explosion and its aftermath. The following excerpt recalls the experiences of Reverend Kiyoshi Tanimoto, pastor of the local Methodist Church.

He was the only person making his way into the city; he met hundreds and hundreds who were fleeing, and every one of them seemed to be hurt in some way. The eyebrows of some were burned off and skin hung from their faces and hands. Others, because of pain, held their arms up as if carrying something in both hands. Some were vomiting as they walked. Many were naked or in shreds of clothing...

THE POSTWAR WORLD

Even before World War II was over in Europe, the Allies had begun to plan the continent's future. During their discussions, it had become clear that the democratic Western Allies (Britain and the United States) had little in common with their communist partner, the Soviet Union. Immediately after the war, as the three nations struggled to create a workable framework for peace, the divisions between them grew.

The first major conference to discuss the post-war world took place in February 1945 at Yalta in the Crimea. The main participants were U.S. president Franklin D. Roosevelt, British prime minister Winston Churchill, and the Soviet leader Joseph Stalin. They decided that Germany and its capital, Berlin, would be divided into four zones, each controlled by a separate country (the United States, Britain, the Soviet Union, and France). They also agreed to set up a new peace-keeping organization, the United Nations. In addition, they declared that all of the newly liberated nations had the right to choose their own form of government.

More discussions took place at the July 1945 Potsdam Conference in Germany. By then much had changed. The war in Europe had ended and the Red Army was camped on huge eastern parts of the continent. Roosevelt had been succeeded by Truman, who thought that communism was a threat

POSTWAR EUROPE

- Territory annexed by the Soviet Union 1940-45
- Territory under Soviet control by 1948
- "Iron Curtain"
- Other countries with Communist governments

to the West. New British prime minister Clement Attlee replaced Churchill halfway through the conference. Some decisions were reached under these difficult conditions, such as determining the future borders of Poland and the establishing of war crimes trials. However, the wish of the Soviet Union to stop free elections in Eastern Europe caused serious clashes.

After Potsdam, the stresses in the relationship between the Soviet Union and its former allies increased, as Stalin imposed his will on one East

The "Big Three" — Winston Churchill, Franklin D. Roosevelt, and Joseph Stalin — at the Yalta Conference in February 1945

European state after another. In 1946, Churchill declared that an "Iron Curtain" — a divide between democratic West and communist East — had descended across the continent. By 1948, Bulgaria, Hungary, Romania, Poland, and Czechoslovakia were all under Soviet control. Communists were also in power in Albania and Yugoslavia.

In 1947, President Truman moved to counteract the Soviet threat. In March, he declared his intention to support any country trying to resist communist rule. This declaration was later called the Truman Doctrine. It stated, "It must be the policy of the United States to support free peoples who are resisting attempted subjugation by armed minorities or by outside pressure." Although no direct mention of communism is made, the reference is clear. Concerned that Europe's post-war economic problems would lead even nations such as France and Italy to embrace communism, Truman also set up the Marshall Plan. This $17 billion aid package was named after U.S. secretary of state George C. Marshall.

The two sides had staked their claims. Their battles were political and intellectual, not physical. The era of the Cold War had begun.

WAR REFUGEES

After the war, many refugees swept across Europe. Millions had fled in front of the advancing Allied armies. Millions more Germans had been driven out of the liberated territories. There were also many Poles, who had lost their lands to Russia in the east. Jews who had survived the death camps and slave laborers who had worked in German factories all struggled to find their way back to their different homelands. The cost in human misery was high.

Hungarian refugees make their way home from Slovakia, where they had worked as slave laborers for the Nazis.

In his memoirs, Field Marshal Viscount Bernard Montgomery (see page 21) details the many problems that faced the Allied armies in Germany after the fighting had ended, in particular the presence of millions of refugees.

After the war, Berliners struggled to repair bomb damage in their city.

In the area occupied by 21 Army Group there were appalling civilian problems to be solved. Over 1 million civilian refugees had fled into the area before the advancing Russians. About 1 million German wounded were in hospital in the area, with no medical supplies. Over 1.5 million unwounded German fighting men had surrendered to 21 Army Group on the 5th May and were now prisoners of war... Food would shortly be exhausted. The transport and communication services had ceased to function, and industry and agriculture were largely at a standstill. The population had to be fed, housed and kept free of disease. It was going to be a race for time whether this could be achieved before the winter began...

CONCLUSION

World War II outdid even World War I in its scope and brutality. The fighting raged across six continents and killed up to sixty million people, more of them civilians than soldiers. More than one third of the casualties came from just one country, Russia. The atrocity of the Holocaust added another inhuman dimension to the conflict.

In the aftermath, the world was transformed. The United States and Russia took their places as the new superpowers and confronted each other in the Cold War for the next forty years. Britain, France, Germany and many other European countries rebuilt their ruined cities and economies with the help of Marshall Aid. Japan slowly recovered from the loss of its empire to become an economically powerful nation. Many Jews left Europe to make homes in Israel, which was established in 1948.

Today the war is still remembered and its effects are still felt. Many of those who fought in the conflict attend annual services of remembrance, and sometimes return to the battle zones. Slave laborers who worked for the Nazis are still fighting to get compensation from the German government.

Jewish organizations continue to track down the few surviving concentration camp officials and high-ranking Nazis who have escaped justice. The Japanese are still suffering the dreadful consequences of the atomic bombs dropped on Hiroshima and Nagasaki. For these people, the war remains a constant part of life.

Since World War II, there have been hundreds of armed conflicts around the world, but none on the same scale. The United Nations, established in 1945 to preserve peace (see document), still works to prevent a repetition of that terrible event, which cost so many millions of lives and ruined many more.

In 1961, a wall was built through Berlin to separate the communist east of the city from the democratic, capitalist west. The wall became a symbol of the Cold War. In the same way, its destruction in 1989 (below) was a sign that this bitter conflict was coming to an end.

Austrian Nazi Adolf Eichmann played a major part in the attempted extermination of the Jews. He disappeared after the war, but was discovered and captured by Israeli agents in 1960. A year later he stood trial in Israel for his war crimes, was found guilty, and was executed.

Many soldiers who participated in World War II remember it with mixed emotions. Often they were fighting for what they believed was right, yet still found it terrible to kill and maim their fellow humans. In these excerpts, British soldier James Bramwell and Jewish American surgeon Dr. Alex Shulman express their thoughts on the conflict. The second extract comes from *The Good War* (see page 37).

When he was mounting his final defense, Hitler recruited boys and old men into his armies because there were not enough men of fighting age left.

I shudder at the thought of war, but men are more evil than I had realised... War is the crunch of big ideas and taking sides is terribly difficult. But it has to be done; and you have to have the idea as you take your side, you're going to prevail. You have to be sure yours is the right side. They are almost religious decisions... War is a kind of uplift to some people. In war you see humanity at the end of its tether, so you know what the human being is capable of. I had moments of feeling cheerful. I wasn't wasting four years of my life.

I'm glad I participated. I felt that whatever little I did was something. My job was to save lives. I was asked, How could you take care of those Germans? Doesn't that bother you? Oh, I started looking at them at first as Germans and Nazis. Then I started looking at them as victims. **Especially at the end, when I saw the kids and the old men.** Could I blame that kid for what his parents or the Nazi leaders did? It was a terrible, mixed feeling. Why shouldn't I take care of a sixteen-year-old kid that's been shot to pieces?

The following excerpt is taken from the Charter of the United Nations, which was adopted on June 25, 1945.

The United Nations building in New York City

We the Peoples of the United Nations determined
   to save succeeding generations from the scourge of war, which twice in our lifetime has brought untold sorrow to mankind, and
   to reaffirm faith in fundamental human rights, in the dignity and worth of the human person, in the equal rights of men and women and of nations large and small...
and for these ends
   to practice tolerance and live together in peace with one another as good neighbors, and
   to unite our strength to maintain international peace and security, and
   to ensure, by the acceptance of principles and the institution of methods, that armed force shall not be used, save in the common interest...
have resolved to combine our efforts to accomplish these aims

GLOSSARY

Afrika Korps The German army that served in North Africa from February 1941 to May 1943.

Allies The forty-nine countries that fought together against the Axis Powers. The main Allies were Great Britain, France, the United States and Russia. Many British Commonwealth countries, such as Australia and India, also fought on the Allied side.

annex To add a territory to one's own land by using military force.

Anschluss The annexation of Austria by the Nazis in 1938.

anti-Semitism Prejudice against and persecution of Jews.

appeasement The policy of giving in to the demands of a potential enemy in an effort to maintain peace.

armistice An official agreement made between opposing sides to stop fighting in a war.

Aryan A member of a supposed white race that the Nazis thought was superior to all others.

Axis Powers The eight countries that fought together against the Allies. The main Axis Powers were Germany and Italy, who formed the Rome-Berlin Axis in 1936, and Japan, who signed the Tripartite Pact with them in 1940.

Balkans A peninsula in southeastern Europe that in World War II contained the countries of Albania, Bulgaria, Greece, Romania, Yugoslavia, and the European part of Turkey.

Blitzkrieg ("lightning war") A Nazi method of attack, designed to overwhelm enemies with its speed and force. It usually began with paratroop drops and air raids, then continued with tank and infantry invasions.

British Expeditionary Force The first British troops that went to France to participate in the war.

capitalism An economic system in which businesses are owned and run by private individuals for their own profit, and not owned by the state.

Central Powers The countries that fought against the Allies in World War I. They were Austria-Hungary, Germany, the Ottoman (Turkish) Empire, and Bulgaria.

chancellor The head of the German government.

coalition government A government made up of more than one political party.

communism A political and economic system whose goal is to create a classless society in which everyone has a fair share of money and power. Communist countries are ruled by members of one political party, who are not elected. Communist businesses are run by the state rather than by private individuals.

concentration camps Camps where large numbers of people were held prisoner. In some Nazi concentration camps, such as Auschwitz and Treblinka, about six million Jews, as well as many gypsies, homosexuals and political prisoners, were killed in gas chambers.

conscription Compulsory service in the armed forces.

convoys A group of merchant ships escorted by navy warships for protection from U-boat attacks.

coup A violent overthrow of a government.

democracy A form of government in which citizens vote to elect their political leaders.

Eastern Front The areas of Eastern Europe where opposing armies fought each other during World War I and World War II.

Entente Cordiale ("friendly understanding") The agreement reached between Britain and France in 1904.

fascism A political belief characterized by extreme nationalism, strong leadership and opposition to both democracy and communism.

Freikorps Groups of men who acted as security forces in Germany after World War I.

front An area of a battle zone where opposing troops face and fight one another directly.

Führer ("leader") The title adopted by Adolf Hitler in 1934.

Gestapo The Nazi secret police force, set up in 1933. The name is short for Geheime Staatspolizei, which means "Secret State Police."

ghettos The areas in European cities such as Warsaw where the Nazis forced Jews to live.

Great Depression The period of high unemployment and economic weakness after the Wall Street Crash of 1929.

Holocaust The mass murder of about six million Jews by the Nazis.

inflation A continued rise in prices of all goods and services.

internment Holding in custody, as in a prison or camp.

Lebensraum ("living space") The term used by Hitler to describe the territories that he occupied, claiming that they provided the space necessary for German people to flourish.

Maginot Line A line of forts and other defenses built by the French, primarily along the German border from Switzerland to Luxembourg.

mandate A conquered territory governed by a member country of the League of Nations.

mobilize To assemble (troops) and prepare them for military action.

Nazi Party The National Socialist German Workers' Party. "Nazi" is a short form of the German words for "National Socialist."

Nazi-Soviet Pact An agreement signed by Germany and Russia in 1939 in which they promised not to attack each other.

Pact of Steel The official military alliance signed by Germany and Italy in May 1939.

paratroopers Troops that drop into battle zones by parachute.

plebiscite A direct vote taken by all the people of a country to decide on an issue of national importance.

purge An act of eliminating political and other opponents, often by murdering them.

putsch A swift and violent revolt, usually designed to overthrow a government.

Red Army The Russian army, so called because it fought under the country's red flag.

Reichstag The name given to both the German parliament and its headquarters.

reparations Compensation, especially the compensation for World War I demanded from Germany in the Treaty of Versailles.

Rome-Berlin Axis The unwritten alliance between Italy under Mussolini and Nazi Germany that began in 1936. It was officially confirmed when the two countries signed the Pact of Steel in 1939.

sanctions Actions taken against a state to punish it for illegal conduct or to force it to act in a certain way, such as a ban on or reduction of exports.

Second Front The European fighting front that opened in France in June 1944, following Operation Overlord.

Serbs A Slavic people who speak Serbo-Croatian.

Slavs A group of peoples from eastern Europe and northwest Asia who speak Slavonic languages such as Russian, Polish and Serbo-Croatian.

SS A Nazi security force led by Heinrich Himmler. Its name is short for the German word *Schutzstaffel*, which means "protection squad." The special *Waffen-SS* fought on the front lines.

strategic bombing Air raids designed to bomb specific targets as part of a wartime strategy.

Sturmabteilung (SA) ("storm division") The Nazis' private terrorist army, led until 1934 by Ernst Röhm. Its members were known as Brownshirts because of their uniforms.

tactical bombing Aerial bombing designed to support attacks by troops on the ground.

Third Reich Germany from 1933 to 1945. The Nazis believed that theirs was the third German Reich (empire) because it followed the Holy Roman Empire of the Middle Ages and the second empire of 1871-1918.

Tripartite Pact The pact signed by Germany, Italy, and Japan in September 1940, in which they agreed to defend one another in case of enemy attack. Romania, Bulgaria and Yugoslavia joined the pact later.

Triple Alliance The alliance formed by Austria-Hungary, Germany and Italy in 1882.

Triple Entente The alliance formed by Britain, France, and Russia in 1907, during the years leading to World War I.

Untermenschen The German word for "subhumans." The Nazis used it to refer to people that they considered inferior, such as Jews and Slavs.

Weimar Republic The republic that existed in Germany from 1919-1933, so called because its government first met in the town of Weimar.

Western Allies Britain, the United States and other World War II Allies from Western capitalist countries.

Western Front The areas of Western Europe where opposing armies fought each other during World War I and World War II.

INDEX